The Power of Forgiveness

By
Martha L. Crockett

Airleaf Publishing

airleaf.com

© Copyright 2006, Martha L. Crockett

All Rights Reserved.

No part of this book may be reproduced, stored in a retrieval system, or transmitted by any means, electronic, mechanical, photocopying, recording, or otherwise, without written permission from the author.

ISBN: 1-59453-627-9

Unless otherwise indicated, all scripture quotations are taken from the King James Version of the Bible. ©Copyright 1979, 1980, 1982 by Thomas Nelson, Inc. Used by permission. All rights reserved.

Scripture quotations marked (NIV) are taken from the New International Version. ©Copyright in 1973, 1978, 1984 by International Bible Society. Used by permission. All rights reserved.

THIS BOOK IS DEDICATED…

To the countless number of people who are suffering from deep hurts and pains and need a word of encouragement.

To the pastors, co-pastors, and first ladies who are triumphant in spite of the many wounds they have received in the ministry.

To the people who are held captive in abusive relationships and to individuals who are involved in the ministry of healing those who are hurting.

ACKNOWLEDGEMENTS

Much gratitude goes to my husband, pastor, and best friend, Herman. Thank you for inspiring me, through your life revolutionizing messages, to attempt to write this book. Thank you for your love, patience, and support. I love you and I am grateful for your editing contributions and ideas, but more importantly, your prayers.

Special thanks to my daughter Tabitha Robertson for editing and reediting. I appreciate your invaluable advice. You are our gift from God. Also, I thank my son-in-law, Kenneth who has so generously allowed you the time to work on this project with me. We love you Kenneth.

Also, to my daughter, 1LT Sheree Gilbert, even though you are miles away, your prayers are appreciated. Thank you for listening to my ideas. You are truly God's gift to your father and me.

My heartfelt appreciation goes to my daughter, Mikela who is now matriculating at the College of William and Mary. Thank you for your editing contributions and encouragement. You too, are a gift from God.

I thank my dear friend, Stephanie Gant, who also inspired me to begin writing. Thank you for your prayers, editing contributions, encouragement, and invaluable advice.

Doretha Smith and Carrie Crenshaw, I appreciate your editing contributions and dedication, which provided me with the time I needed to work on this book.

Also, a sincere gratitude to Ernestine Smith whose commitment provided me the time I needed to complete this work.

Thanks to Brian and Tina Schaeffer for their technological contributions.

I thank my special friend Mary Johnson who has been instrumental in my writing of this book in a very special way.

Many thanks to the members of Faith and Hope Temple Church of God in Christ (COGIC) who have been supportive of this ministry. May God bless each of you.

TABLE OF CONTENTS

INTRODUCTION xiii

CHAPTER I: A MATRIARCH OF PAIN 1

CHAPTER II: A DAUGHTER OF A MATRIARCH OF PAIN 10

CHAPTER III: THE IMPACT OF PAIN 15

    Inner Pain Accomplishing God's Purpose 15

    Pain Causes Action and Reaction 17

    Another Dimension of Pain 21

    Past Hurts Hinder Present Performance 25

    Inner Pain Will Make You Bitter or Better 32

CHAPTER IV: A REMEDY FOR INNER HEALING 38

    Why Forgiveness is Necessary 38

    A Revelation Unfolds 41

    What It Means to Forgive and Forget 43

    Grace Helps Us to Forgive the Unforgivable 48

    The Danger of Walking in Unforgiveness 50

CHAPTER V: CHANNELS OF BLESSINGS AND CURSES 56

CHAPTER VI: ANGER IS DANGEROUS 61

The Importance of Mastering Anger...................... 61

How To Manage Anger 62

The Impact of God's Anger 64

CHAPTER VII: A CRITICAL ANALYSIS TO INNER HEALING.......................... 70

(1) Determine That You Are Hurting................... 70

(2) Determine What Caused the Hurt................... 73

(3) Determine Your Alternatives and Select Your Best Choice... 73

(4) Prayerfully Implement Your Choice............... 75

CHAPTER VIII: THE HEALING POWER OF A DISCIPLINED PRAYER LIFE..... 76

CHAPTER IX: THE HEALING POWER OF THE WORD AND THE BLOOD 79

The Healing Power of God's Word 79

There is Healing in the Blood of Jesus 83

CHAPTER X: RISE-UP AND DELIVER YOURSELF 85

In Conclusion.. 88

CHAPTER XI: PERSONAL TESTAMONIES OF HOW I FOUND COMFORT IN THE WORD OF GOD THROUGH PRAYER.... 90

APPENDIX 95
  Self Development Activities 95

INTRODUCTION

During the course of my life, I have endured much inner pain. As a result, I have come to understand what it means to be emotionally wounded. More importantly, I have experienced glorious victories through the power of forgiveness.

Perhaps you too have suffered inner hurt in your life. If so, you are not alone. The ability to feel emotional pain is a human characteristic, and many people will eventually undergo it at some season in life. It does not matter who we are; our religious persuasion is irrelevant. We may be Catholic or Protestant. We may practice Buddhism, Hinduism, or choose to be an Atheist. We may be rich or poor, black or white, but inner pain will remind us that we are mere mortals, and it will make us conscience of the reality that we are not supreme beings. In fact, emotional hurt helps us to realize that someone or something, other than ourselves, is in control of our destiny.

Inner pain can be torturing and sometimes unbearable; there have been people who have asked to die; others have committed suicide. To experience pain of this magnitude may be the result of anger, bitterness, or resentment that develops when we harbor unforgiveness. If you have been very deeply wounded, and you are still in pain, more than likely, it is because you have not been able to forgive. When we forgive, it releases us from the bondage of emotional torment. Therefore, when we have endured excruciating inner hurt, it is of utmost importance that during the course of time we let go and begin to experience inner healing. Otherwise, we may become overwhelmed with additional hurt that will affect our total being.

Healing of your emotional self must be dealt with through the inner man. One cannot treat it from the outside because the cure for inner pain deals with the internal you. Is there an earthly surgeon skillful enough to extract an emotional hurt? Is there a wonder drug that has the potency to cure this insidious disease? At any rate, we must control this plaguing epidemic, or it will control us. If we don't master it, it will master us; if it is not dealt with appropriately, it will result in a more grievous and painful end. However, the end does not have to be neither grievous or painful.

Inner hurt can become an awesome testimony of healing and deliverance. It has the ability to make one better instead of bitter. The effects of our emotional traumas can serve as the evidence that they can make us, and not necessarily break us. In other words, God may use our painful experiences to make us what He has already intended for us to be, and to take us where He has already intended for us to go. In actuality, what the devil devises for our harm, God is able to use it, and make it work for our good.

Our Heavenly Father has graciously provided for the healing of all that are hurting; there is a balm for your inward distress. You can find it in the word of God, and it can be obtained through prayer. When you apply this remedy to your particular situation, it will cause miraculous things to take place in your life. If you are hurting, or know of someone who is, I hope and pray that you will discover the reason for the pain and the pathway to deliverance. As you travel with me through the trials and triumphs of others, perhaps you will discover the impact of harboring anger, bitterness, and resentment, and the devastation we encounter when we fail to forgive.

While turning the pages of this book, I trust you will notice how I came to know the healing and delivering power of forgiveness; in doing so, you too will be able to experience a wonderful and victorious life. It is not an isolated incident; it is available to all of God's children.

CHAPTER I: A MATRIARCH OF PAIN

It appears that some people were born to endure pain. One such person was my mother. As though it was not enough for her father to walk out of her life at a very young age, her mother died when she was four years old. She was raised by her uncle and his wife. According to my mom, her uncle's wife was far from a loving mother. At the age of seventeen she married my father and the *hurt began to hurt.*

My parents were very hard workers; they were uneducated, but they were survivors. During my formative years, they were sharecroppers living on a plantation in Mississippi. As sharecroppers, we understood at a very young age what hard work was. I was always a very alert child, and I can vividly remember the last year we lived on that farmstead; it was the year I turned ten years old, and my oldest living brother at that time, who is now deceased, was eight.

During the late fall of 1957, my father's brother hit him in his head, and he suffered a terrible injury which rendered him unable to work. My brother and I basically chopped the cotton for our family's crop in the year of 1958. Since we had not cleared any money from the fall of 1957, my mom and oldest sister had to work in another field to make money for the family to live on during that year.

Martha L. Crockett

I can very clearly recall my father telling my mother that we did not get any money at the end of the harvest after settlement with the boss. Consequently, we not only learned what it meant to work hard, but we also learned what it meant to work hard, and not receive any money. Of course, my father said he was told that our money had been used up during the year.

I never understood what it was used for, I only knew we did not get any. The only bills I know we had to pay out of our settlement were for the shabby cold house we lived in and doctor bills. Over a span of four years, one of my brothers had to go to the doctor because his nose bled for a half-day. Since it would not stop bleeding, my father had to get permission from the boss to take my brother to the doctor. I remember my oldest sister going to the doctor only once when she was pregnant, and my mother went once when she became pregnant. Those were the only times I remember anyone in our household going to the doctor over that four-year span. However, when my father had that terrible life-threatening blow to his head, he had hospital and doctor bills; of course those bills would have come out of the 1958 settlement. Before the settlement, we moved to Arkansas. My father's mother orchestrated our move, but I believe it was divinely ordered by God.

My father was a very quiet man. He worked hard during the week. I believe, as a result of much inner hurt, on the weekend whenever he got paid the little money for working in other people's fields, he would use it to get drunk. Even though we had very little to no money, he found a way to get corn whisky. Whenever he got a little corn whisky, he would become very physically, mentally, and verbally abusive, but he never physically abused us as small children. However, when he would come home with his abusive behavior toward Mom, I would always get a strange feeling that I could not understand.

On the weekends, we never knew when dad was going to come home, and we never knew what he was going to do. Of course, we had become accustomed to being prepared to run away from the house whenever he came. My mom would get a blanket to spread over us while we slept in the cotton patch or in the barn next to where the horses were kept. I never knew how my other siblings felt about what we *heard* and *saw* because we *never,* talked about it; I don't know why we didn't. However, after forty-five years, upon commencing to write this book, I dared to speak to them about their feelings. As for me, sleeping in the fields and barn was an adventurous time, since that was basically the only excitement around our house. This was basically a typical weekend for the four years we lived on that particular plantation. However, I do remember going into the town about three or four times during that four-year span. I also remember visiting some of our other relatives occasionally, and of course, they visited us.

Martha L. Crockett

After moving to Arkansas, my mother did domestic work and my oldest sister worked in a restaurant to take care of the family because my father was still disabled. His condition grew worse, and it caused him much mental anguish; my mother became even more afraid of him. He spent months in the mental hospital. After a couple of episodes, my mom decided not to continue living in those conditions. I could not understand why she could not let us all stay together. When we discussed it, she told me that she had been out in the deep waters, and had finally gotten to the bank. Also, she said she had suffered too much for so long and that I did not understand. My mother also said that she did not feel like she had to continue to put up with the abuse any more.

For twenty years, she had endured heart-wrenching abuse. I remember the last time my mother had an encounter with my father; he had just come home from the hospital. I recall him running her out of the house; she ran across the road into some bushes; my brother and I ran behind them. I felt something terrible was about to happen. We had never gotten involved before; I guess we were too young. This particular night, we intercepted the altercation. A gentleman who was our neighbor saw us, and he helped us carry our mom into his house. He and his wife put her on their bed. She looked so pitiful; I touched her, but I got scared because her skin was clammy, and I thought she was going to die. The strange thing was that our dad never touched us. He went back into the house. Some time later Mom came home. I was about eleven years old at that time.

After everything I saw, as a child growing up, I was still a daddy's girl. I loved both of my parents very much, but I did not understand the abuse that my mother suffered; nor did I understand that my siblings and I were also being emotionally and mentally abused as well. Hence, I became angry when Mom left Dad. I felt as though she was the cause of the broken family, and I wanted all of us to stay together. While we were poor and poverty stricken, we had each other, and that was the most important thing to me. Nevertheless, as I became an adult, I understood why my mom had to leave. Although, I came to understand it as an adult, I resented it as a child.

I suppose I resented my mother's actions because she had allowed us to stay in that type of atmosphere during our formative years, and I had become comfortable with such a lifestyle. Of course, since no one ever came to her rescue, she had no way out, and nowhere to go. As a young child, other than feeling funny when my dad became abusive, I really did not know that his behavior was all that bad. Sometimes, our neighbors would stand on their porches and just watch what was going on at our house. For me, all of this just seemed to have been a way of life. My mother was a good woman. My father was a good person too, but I believe he had some deep wounds. They both were victims of their environment.

Martha L. Crockett

My grandmother and step grandfather loved me dearly, and I loved them too, but perhaps the environment they cultivated for my father contributed to some of his behavior. My dad's mom and step dad worked very hard during the week. On the weekends they would get together with other people to drink, fuss, cuss, and talk very badly to and about each other. Sometimes during those gatherings, they would intimidate one another with guns. I suppose that's why my father became a weekend drinker and abuser. Maybe there were some other factors also. Whatever reason lead to his conduct, it cost him his health and his family.

I recall my grandmother would often buy me a new dress or something, but she never bought my other siblings anything. Later, I learned that my mom did not like her making that difference in us, but she could not say anything. At that time, I was excited because that was the only time I got a new dress except the one time when I was about four or five years old; I got a new dress for Mother's Day. The only other time I remember getting a new dress was when I was ten years old. My dad's father who was a minister of the gospel bought it for my baptism; actually he dressed me from head to toe. My mother made, out of flour sacks, all of the other dresses *I got up to age ten. (*Flour sacks were the pretty print cloth bags our flour came in).

The Power of Forgiveness

My mom passed away at the age of sixty-three. Of course, I had resolved my anger many years before she died. I was angry with her because I felt she was the only one who could have kept our family together; but I could not fathom, at that time, what it could have cost her. My mom was aware of the fact that I did not want her to leave Dad; however, she did not know that I held her responsible for the family being broken. As an adult, I shared my childhood feelings with her. She was very hurt that I had felt that way. Little did I know, the family was already broken many years before my mom left.

As an adolescent, I was angry with my mother; at some point in my life I forgave her for what I felt was an unforgivable hurt. I don't remember when the hurt stopped hurting, but I know I stopped being angry with her. Before my mom passed away, we were the best of friends. She lived in my house the last four years of her life. In fact, at one time when she was living with us, she told me that my husband and I had been more than children to her; she said we had been like a father and mother. I will remember those words as long as I have my ability to think.

Also, I will never forget the big smile that came across her face after enduring more than twelve hours of surgery. Her face and head appeared to have been swollen twice its normal size. When I asked her how she was doing, in spite of her exhausting condition, she smiled and said; *"I'm fine."* She never complained about her situation. For one month, the nurses awakened her every hour or so to irrigate her incision in an effort to control the overwhelming infection. In the end, she did tell me she was tired. I suppose so, after having her sleep disturbed nearly every hour on the hour for more than a month.

While she endured much inner pain as a child, wife, and young mother she always seemed to have been able to bring sunshine to others. Even during her senior years, as she was undergoing her most painful physical suffering of colon cancer, she had a way of lighting up a room with her smile. Not even the pangs of cancer could wipe it off of her face.

I often questioned God as to why my mother endured so much pain. At times, I have felt that life was unfair to her. She was always nice, even to people who hurt her. She was kind as she endured some of her most agonizing hurt. Nevertheless, after God revealed the reason for some of the hurt she encountered, I resolved that everything had a purpose. Nevertheless, somehow in the midst of her bittersweet life, she was a champion of a Christian; she faced death courageously as though she was its equal. In the end when I asked her if she was scared, without hesitation she said, "No I'm not scared." Truly she was a matriarch of pain. Through all of her experiences, she never became bitter. As far as forgiveness is concerned, she taught me how to live, and in the end she taught me how to die.

This section is dedicated to my loving mother. Only God and you really knew the magnitude of your hurt. Your life has been an inspiration to me and has served as an instrument by which I have been able to understand what it means to hurt and to forgive.

CHAPTER II: A DAUGHTER OF A MATRIARCH OF PAIN

Of all my adverse memories of the plantation life in Mississippi, the very last experience I had, was the day I got baptized on Sunday, August 10, 1958. My grandmother was very determined to get us away from that plantation. Therefore, I left the riverside where I got baptized; I went into an old house and put on my new clothes that my grandfather bought for my baptism; I got into a parked car that was waiting for me, and we headed to Arkansas that very same hour. By God's providence, I had attended a revival every night during the last week we lived on that farm; this was the first time I could ever remember attending a revival. During that week, as a 10-year old girl, I sat on the *Mourners' Bench* every night, and I prayed with all of my being for Jesus to come into my heart. I did not know how to pray; I just said what my mother had taught me. I suppose because she was so wounded herself, she did not verbally teach me a lot about *life,* but she did teach me my most invaluable lesson. I learned from my mother that Jesus loved and died for me. She also taught me that I needed Jesus in my life, and I became determined to have him. On Friday, August 8th of the revival, in the little old country church, Jesus *really* came into my heart.

The Power of Forgiveness

I did not think about it then, but I know now why it was imperative for me to have Jesus as I faced my new life in the city. I understand why the Holy Ghost moved upon me with a burning desire to attend the revival my last week on the plantation. For a reason unknown to me at that time, I felt something drawing me to those services; I had just turned 10 years old, but I had to go. It has been my faith in Jesus that has kept me stable down through the years. It was his love that caused a supernatural happening to take place in my family that incited my dad and my mom to send me to the revival per my request. It was unusual because it seemed that my dad was more eager for me to go to those meetings than my mom was. He was convalescing from his head injury; my mom had just had a new baby; therefore, my oldest sister walked me to the revival every night.

While living on the plantation in Mississippi, we went to school about three or four months out of the year. I clearly remember the two-room schoolhouse, and the principal, who was my teacher. I recall one school day when I was 9 years old, and yes, I was in the first grade. I did not have a spelling book, so I went to my teacher and asked for one. She searched through her boxes, but she could not find a 1st grade speller. So, she handed me the 2nd grade speller, and said, "Here; you are in the 2nd grade." At that time, I couldn't read or spell the words in the 1st grade book. At the age of 9, I remember Mrs. Wells calling out spelling words to the children. When she would get to me, I could not spell anything. I could not spell simple words such as *I, he, it, me, so,* and *etc.* Perhaps if there had been Special Education when I was in school, I would have been placed in that program.

The first day that I was to attend school in Arkansas, I was already ten years old and in the 2nd grade. I was very apprehensive about going to the unfamiliar environment. I wanted to read so badly. I didn't want the feeling of embarrassment I so often had when I was unable to spell or read in the school in Mississippi. My dad could not read either, but I vividly recall the night before I was to go to the new school. He must have known exactly how I felt; he sat with me late into the night and tried to help me to read from the textbook he had gotten from the new school. He also, got up early the next morning, and again he tried to help me with my reading. He was very bright, and he remembered some of the words that my mom had read to us earlier, and he kept going over them with me.

On my first day at the new school, when the time came, *Believe It or Not,* I stumbled through the paragraph the teacher asked me to read. The book I read from was about a bear named *Smokey.* After that, I felt very good inside. I did not feel the way I had felt in the two-room schoolhouse in Mississippi. The next day when I went to school, the strangest thing happened, I read my paragraph like a champion, and I have been reading every since. Also, for some strange reason that I never thought about back then, I learned

The Power of Forgiveness

how to spell just as fast as I had learned to read. By the end of six months when my teacher, Mrs. Green, had her spelling class, when she would get to me, she would say, "It's no need of wasting time with Marthalean, we know she knows how to spell all of the words."

In retrospect, basically, I learned to read in one night. As a child, I thought this was great; as an adult, I realized it was unusual. Upon commencing to write this book, I conferred with a psychiatrist. I was informed that a phenomenon of this nature is more than likely related to the environment. When children live in a poverty stricken environment, inundated with various forms of abuse, it has the potential to cause mental blocks, in essence, hindering their ability to learn.

As a child, I never received a psychological evaluation: nonetheless, I believe my problem was of an environmental nature. In spite of it all, I give God praise because this experience has been instrumental in accomplishing my mission of ministering to those that are hurting. Some children laughed at me because I was three years behind in my grade. Consequently, I know what it feels like to have children to tease you because you are three years behind. I know the feeling of being humiliated in school because you can't read or spell at the age of 9. I know what it feels like to have children pick on you because you are poor and can't buy your lunch. Even if you walked home to get lunch, the only food you have is rice and butter from the commodity program that is contaminated by the rats and roaches in your house. I know what it feels like to go to school with the stench of urine because you are unable to control your bladder during the night. It does not matter how hard you try and how much your parents fuss and say, "You are too lazy to get up;" you just can't stop wetting in the bed. (At the time, I did not realize, because during that time, no one told me, I needed to wash. I was only told that I was *stinky*.) I know what children go through when they are laughed at because of their hygiene and clothes. I even know what it feels like to have your teacher embarrass you before the class because of your hygiene. I know what it feels like for your dad to have to walk you to school because certain children harass and double-team you because they don't like you because of where you come from. (In fact, some children nicknamed me *Mississippi.*) I know what it means to have children joke on you and your family because of where you live. *It hurts, but while it may hurt, it can heal.*

If you are experiencing pain relative to school, either past or present, please remember, it is not where you are now, but it is where you can go. You are not accountable for your beginning, but you are definitely responsible for your end. It is not who your parents are, but it is who your maker is. It is not the experiences, but it is how you embrace them. Therefore, don't become bitter with the world and retaliate by trying to overcome your hurt by hurting others. Arise and take hold of God's hand; He is ready to heal your hurt, just as He healed mine.

CHAPTER III: THE IMPACT OF PAIN

Inner Pain Accomplishing God's Purpose

There is a story in the book of Genesis that provides much insight into the impact inner pain can have on its victims. Also, it reveals that God has the divine ability to use our emotional hurts and make them work for our good. This story gives an account of a young lad named Joseph, who was placed in a tormenting situation by his very own brothers. Joseph's father loved him more than any of his children and made him a coat of many colors. Joseph's brothers became jealous and made plans to kill him. Rueben, one of the brothers, discouraged this; so instead, they stripped him of his coat and put him into a pit where there was no water. By an act of divine providence, they eventually sold Joseph to a caravan of Ishmaelites traveling to Egypt. An account of Joseph's perception of his experience is found in Genesis 45:4-5:

And Joseph said unto his brethren, Come near to me, I pray you. And they came near. And he said I am Joseph your brother, whom Ye sold into Egypt.

Now therefore be not grieved, nor angry with yourselves, that ye sold me hither: for God did send me before you to preserve life.

Like Joseph, whenever we as Christians experience inner pain, it should be viewed as a means of accomplishing God's purpose and plan in our lives. When we understand that God is always working in every situation that we encounter, it should help us to see the good in it. Also, in spite of what we feel, it should aid us in realizing that we must bring the best out of every emotional hurt, and it will bring the best out of us. Therefore, look for the good in every painful circumstance, and it will make you a better person. It may be tormenting, but it can bring you into an emotional and spiritual maturity. Joseph understood that God caused everything he experienced to work for his good; as a result, he was able to entreat his brothers with kindness when they came to him for food during the time of famine. I am not sure how long it took Joseph to get to this point; he was a young lad when they sold him into Egypt; however, he was an adult when he entreated them as a ruler in Pharaoh's house. The most important thing is that he was able to see God working in the midst of his atrocity.

While we may not always see anything good in our adversities, by faith we must know that *it's in there,* and somehow, it is working together to bring something marvelous out of us. To better understand how all of our experiences work together for our good, imagine a cake in process. First, none of the individual raw ingredients are very tasty when eaten alone. For example, flour is bland; oil is oily; and the other dry ingredients, along with various other flavors are nothing

The Power of Forgiveness

really special when consumed by themselves. Nevertheless, when all of these single ingredients are mixed together, and put through a baking process, the goal of the end product is a scrumptious, prize-winning cake.

In like manner, as a result of *the good, the bad, the beautiful, and the ugly,* God allows us to go through the process of experiencing hurt and pain. We must understand that all of these experiences work together in order to make something wonderful out of us, and we must realize that in some way God's purpose is being accomplished. Sometimes, when we are going through, it feels like we are not going to make it to the other side of our pain; we feel like giving up. It may seem as though the pain is unfair and appears that it will be a permanent part of our existence. During these times, God's children may need to be reminded that all things are working together for their good. At these junctions in life, we will need the mighty power of God to keep us in character. More importantly, we need the power of God to work in us to pull down the strongholds in our lives. As we submit to the will of God, even when we do not understand what is happening, in spite of our encounters, God will apply His grace to our situation and enable us to live victoriously.

Pain Causes Action and Reaction

Normally, a person does not readily embrace pain; however, it has a positive side. From a physical perspective, if we could not feel it, we could be dying, unknowingly, of some terrible condition. Pain causes action and reaction and lets us know that we have feelings; it makes us aware that we are alive, and to some extent that we are in touch with reality. In spite of this, it does not matter how positive it may be, we might not take pleasure in the discomfort it brings. As a result of our reaction to its intensity, we are moved to action. If it becomes unbearable, we might do almost anything to find relief.

As we further observe the impact inner hurt can have on its victims, let us briefly examine the life of another patriarch of pain by the name of Job. The devil knows the impact pain has on its victims; for this reason, he confronted God, and challenged Him to take His protection from around Job. To prove that man would curse God to His face, if subjected to enough pain, Satan asked God for permission to strip Job, a righteous man, of all he had.

With God's divine consent, immediately the devil began to strike Job with one torturous blow after another. First, Satan caused the Sabeans to kill Job's servants and carried all of his cattle away. While a servant was reporting to him what had happened, another report came that lightning had fallen upon and burned up Job's sheep and the servants. As the second servant was giving an account of what had happened, another messenger arrived and told Job that some Chaldeans had stolen all of his camels and killed the

The Power of Forgiveness

servants. As if this were not enough pain, a fourth messenger came while the third was speaking and told Job that a wind had hit the four-corners of the house, and had fallen in on his children, killing them. Upon hearing all of this, Job was moved to action. He got up, tore his clothes, and shaved his head. Nevertheless, instead of cursing God, he bowed down and worshipped Him. Even after loosing all of his earthly possessions and children, Job never blamed nor cursed God; therefore, Satan petitioned God to let him touch Job's body. Satan said that a person would do anything to save his life; after which, he left the Lord's presence and with divine permission, immediately afflicted Job with painful boils from the top of his head to the soles of his feet. Yet, Job remained blameless before God; nonetheless, his overwhelming anguish provoked him to curse the day he was born. Job's verbal expression is indicative of his heart-wrenching experience. The following is an account of his reactions to his agonizing encounters. Job 3: 1-10 reads:

After this opened Job his mouth, and cursed his day.

And Job spake, and said, let the day perish wherein I was born, and the night in which it was said, There is a man-child conceived.

Let that day be darkness; let not God regard it from above, neither let the light shine upon it.

Let darkness and the shadow of death stain it; let a cloud dwell upon it; let the blackness of the day terrify it.

As for that night, let darkness seize upon it; let it not be joined unto the days of the year, let it not come into the number of the months.

Lo, let that night be solitary, let no joyful voice come therein.

Let them curse it that curse the day, who are ready to raise up their mourning.

Let the stars of the twilight thereof be dark; let it look for light, but have none; neither let it see the dawning of the day:

Because it shut not up the doors of my mother's womb, nor hid sorrow from mine eyes.

Job's words provide unparalleled insight into how tormenting experiences can influence behavior. Here was a man who was emotionally and spiritually mature; he feared God and refrained from doing evil. In spite of the loss of his material possessions; the pain of hearing of his children's destruction; and finally, the stroke of tormenting boils covering his entire body created an overwhelming and harrowing situation. Nevertheless, Job declared in chapter 13 and verse 15:

Though he slay me, yet will I trust in him: but I will maintain mine own ways before him.

Job 42:10 tells us that after he had prayed for his friends, the Lord made him prosperous again and gave him twice as much as he had before. The Lord blessed the latter years of Job to be exceedingly better than the beginning and gave him an additional 140 years of life to enjoy. Job's story provides evidence that pain can move one to action and reaction.

Another Dimension of Pain

Usually the paralysis some hurting people experience causes them to have difficulty functioning in certain areas of their lives. When they have been wounded and have not been able to forgive, another dimension of hurt is created both internally and externally. Sometimes, the hurt causes them to be unable to perform for extended periods of time; they try to be dependable, but the hurt prohibits their performance. Also, since they have been so deeply wounded, their ability to relate to others may be greatly inhibited as well. The injury that people have endured as a result of inner pain, often causes them to become unproductive and hurt others because *hurt people, hurt people.*

> As a result of being broken ourselves, we may cause others to be broken. When this happens, it causes us to experience another dimension of pain; it is where *the hurt begins to hurt.*

There are many people who have undergone suffering of this magnitude. Sometimes when a person has been hurt so badly, and has not been able to let go, it can become more painful. As a result, their behavior may become destructive, and they may have a tendency to hurt themselves even more; not only will they hurt themselves, but those who are close to them.

How many good people have found themselves in this kind of situation? How many are living miserably because they are harboring unforgiveness? What some people don't seem to realize is that when they refuse to release others, they usually don't hurt their offenders; they hurt themselves, and perhaps, other innocent people. There are other hurting people who don't seem to understand that they are not responsible for what people do to them, but they are most definitely accountable for the way they respond. Many times we use the phrase "They broke God's commandments," when we refer to someone that has transgressed God's law. According to the Vine's Expository Dictionary of Old and New Testament Words, by W.E. Vine, the word transgress is derived from a Greek word "parabates," which has been translated as "breaker" by

The Power of Forgiveness

some scholars. Practically speaking, "break" means to crack, fracture, or rupture. God's precepts cannot be cracked, fractured, or ruptured as a result of any human behavior. The bible tells us that God's word is settled in heaven forever. God's law is just as in tact today as it was when He gave it to Moses upon Mount Sinai.

When Moses came down from Mount Sinai after having been in communion with God for forty days, he saw the people dancing before the golden calf; Moses became angry and broke the tables on which the Ten Commandments were written. While the tables were broken, God's laws remained in tact. In the same light, when we disobey God's commandments, we break ourselves; we cannot break God's laws. God's word commands us to forgive others. When we choose not to do so, it breaks us. It may break our health, it may break our emotions, it may break our relationships with loved ones, and finally, it will break our relationship with God.

Consequently, pain that is allowed to continue will cause more hurtful experiences. For example, hurt endured as an innocent child can cause excessive emotional damage. As an adult, one may get involved in all kinds of harmful activities that lead to more painful experiences. Behavior as a result of deep pain may drive one to transgress God's law. Nevertheless, the bottom line is this, it does not matter what leads one to disobey God's law; the fact is when we disobey, we break ourselves. As a result of being broken ourselves, we may cause others to be broken. When this happens, it causes us to experience another dimension of pain; it is where *the hurt begins to hurt.*

When *hurt people, hurt people,* they isolate themselves. Usually, they don't want to be separated from the people who really love them, but as a result of their own behavior, they have a tendency to drive others out of their lives and become victims of isolation. Many of them have been robbed of their ability to demonstrate the stability necessary to nurture lasting friendships and relationships. For example, they may turn to drugs or alcohol as a means of coping with their inner pain. Many times, a substance abuser will become an abuser. They may verbally, emotionally, or even physically abuse their spouse, children, friends, and others; when this happens, it may force loved ones to end personal relationships. In some cases, hurting people have had to give up their children because they did not have the capacity to exercise good parenting skills. As a result, this causes them more pain, and they may get involved in other destructive activities.

For example, some women who are deeply wounded may turn to promiscuity as a result of low *self-esteem.* Low self-esteem has lead many beautiful women to feel very bad about themselves, and live lives of immorality. It has caused some to be drawn to men that sexually, mentally, and physically abuse them and then leave them. Often, they do not feel that they deserve better. This lack of self-worth does not affect

The Power of Forgiveness

women only, but men as well. Sometimes, men will sexually, emotionally, and physically abuse a woman or a child because they are suffering from low self-esteem. Consequently, these behaviors, and others, cause hurt people to hurt others. Usually when we are hurt, we have a tendency not to wound only ourselves, but others as well.

Even though you may have been deeply wounded, and your pain has caused you more sorrow and devastation; remember, God wants to bring your mental distress to a victorious end; no matter what you have done, it is not too late; no matter how you feel, God can turn your seemingly impossible situation around. He can deliver you from your addictive behaviors that have brought you loneliness and isolation. If your suffering is a result of your unresolved inner hurts, I submit to you that your inner pain may have turned into emotional bitterness. As a result of your bitterness, you have begun to hurt others, and inadvertently, you have hurt yourself.

Past Hurts Hinder Present Performance

…past hurts may hinder present performance.

Some people exhibit extreme instability when they try to fulfill their obligations. Also, many times they may demonstrate difficulty in relating to others. When this happens, it is usually the result of deep painful experiences that have not been dealt with appropriately. For example, it may be difficult for them to get along with their co-workers. Some may even get joy out of making other people hurt. In essence, some hurt is such that it may affect their overall personality. It may cause them to experience chronic depression, and it may affect how they maintained their continuity in kingdom work. While I may not understand all the dynamics that impact the behavior of people who have experienced very deep wounds, it appears that when issues are not resolved, they will impact various aspects of their lives, hence, hindering their ability to execute their duties effectively. Actually, past hurts may hinder present performance.

As I reflect upon those who are affected by past hurts, I am often reminded of the story of the Samaritan woman who came in contact with Jesus at Jacob's well. The bible does not specifically state that she had past hurts, but as you read her story, you can be certain that she did. There are clues that provide insight into her miserable life. Let's look at John 4: 7-19:

There cometh a woman of Samaria to draw water: Jesus saith unto her, Give me to drink.

(For his disciples were gone away unto the city to buy meat.)

Then saith the woman of Samaria unto him, How is it that thou, being a Jew, askest drink of me, which am a woman of Samaria? for the Jews have no dealings with the Samaritans.

Jesus answered and said unto her, If thou knewest the gift of God, and who it is that saith to thee, Give me to drink; thou wouldest have asked of him, and he would have given thee living water.

The woman saith unto him, Sir, thou hast nothing to draw with, and the well is deep: from whence then hast thou that living water?

Art thou greater than our father Jacob, which gave us the well, and drank thereof himself, and his children, and his cattle?

Jesus answered and said unto her, Whosoever drinketh of this water shall thirst again:

But whosoever drinketh of the water that I shall give him shall never thirst; but the water that I shall give him shall be in him a well of water springing up into everlasting life.

The woman saith unto him, Sir, give me this water, that I thirst not, neither come hither to draw.

Martha L. Crockett

> *Jesus saith unto her, Go, call thy husband, and come hither. The woman answered and said, I have no husband. Jesus said unto her, Thou hast well said, I have no husband:*
>
> *For thou hast had five husbands; and he whom thou now hast is not thy husband: in that saidst thou truly.*
>
> *The woman saith unto him, Sir, I perceive that thou art a prophet.*

This passage introduces to us the woman of Samaria as she meets Jesus at the well. Their dialogue begins when Jesus asks her for a drink of water. She responds to him by asking how could he, being a Jew, ask her a woman of Samaria for a drink of water. The custom was that the Jews were to have no dealings with Samaritans. Jesus does not answer her question directly, but he makes a statement, which created an environment for further dialogue. The conversation eventually provided an opportunity for the woman to make a request.

Finally, she did make a request that proved to be mind-changing, heart-transforming, and life-revolutionizing. "Give me this water." Upon asking Jesus for a drink of living water, he drops the bomb. He drops the bomb that exploded her mind. It held the key to the revelation of her innermost pain; it revealed, perhaps, a source of her deep wounds. This was the

The Power of Forgiveness

beginning of something that would literally revolutionize her life. It was the dynamite that commenced the setting of her soul ablaze. Here was the beginning of a change that transformed her from a sinner into a powerful and influential missionary. Jesus told her, "Go, call thy husband and come here." This is the turning point for something better. She tells Jesus that she has no husband. Jesus replied to her that she had told the truth when she said she had no husband. He follows up with the revelation only God could have made known. "You have had five husbands, and the one that you now have is not your husband." Jesus confirmed that she had told the truth. Here lay the secret to the inner most hurts and pains she had endured.

Imagine, a woman having had five husbands. Her present living arrangement was unwholesome; it appears that she had chosen to live with a man without the benefit of holy matrimony. What could have possibly come out of five broken marriages, and being presently involved in a relationship where there was no pledge of commitment? We know that there was a different experience with six different men. Also, we can be certain that there was *pain, pain, pain, pain, pain* and more *pain*. There are no clues as to the kind of men to whom she had been married; we have no specific insight into their personalities, character, and etc. We can infer that the man with whom she was presently involved was in consent to live with her in an uncommitted relationship.

Martha L. Crockett

The plaguing questions are these: could it be that only the men had issues? Were they totally responsible for the broken marriages? Was this woman the only innocent party? This is hardly the case. Whatever led to so many broken marriages, I am persuaded that she had some unresolved pain, which contributed to this situation as well. It is no doubt that her past experiences had some influence in her present uncommitted relationship. Nevertheless, when she met Jesus, it is obvious that she became a changed woman. He gave her purpose and direction. He empowered her to perform effectively as a missionary. Immediately, she left her water pot and went into the city and told the men, "Come see a man who told me everything I ever did." Whatever pain she had, one encounter with Jesus made a difference in her broken life. It will make a difference in your life too.

What I have seen of people who have been involved in three or more broken marriages are people who usually demonstrate severe past hurts and pains. Their wounds inhibit them from coping with the responsibilities that are required of mature married people. This may not be the case in all situations, but experience has led me to believe that while this scenario may not fit every case, it is exemplary of many that I have seen. Nevertheless, in spite of the pain, an encounter with Jesus can open up a whole new channel of developing wholesome relationships.

The Power of Forgiveness

☀☀☀☀☀☀☀☀☀☀☀☀☀☀☀☀☀☀☀☀☀☀☀☀☀☀☀☀☀☀
> The bible teaches in Matthew 19:4-6 that when two people come together, they are no more twain. In conjunction, I believe, based on my experience, that when broken people come together they have more pain.

☀☀☀☀☀☀☀☀☀☀☀☀☀☀☀☀☀☀☀☀☀☀☀☀☀☀☀☀☀☀

It appears that when deeply hurt people enter into a marriage unit, with broken pieces, they appear to expect their mate to make them happy. To attain and maintain a happy marriage is a shared responsibility. It is not the sole responsibility of one person to ensure happiness in the relationship. Both must work together to ensure that this happens. The bible teaches in Matthew 19:4-6 that when two people come together, they are no more twain. In conjunction, I believe, based on my experience, that when broken people come together they have more pain.

This sheds some light on why there is so much unresolved conflict in a relation where one party has experienced deep inner wounds. If both have inner pain, the consequences are even more severe. When hurt people come together in a marriage, they bring all of their pain, experiences, and dependencies. Usually, they are unable to give and take to the extent that requires balance.

People, who have deep wounds, have a tendency to think of themselves more than they do others. When you think of your needs and desires more than you do your mate's, more than likely, you will sacrifice your spouse's happiness for your own. When you sacrifice your mate's happiness for yours, it causes more unhappiness, conflict, tension, and other related problems. If you have not been able to resolve your inner pain before you enter into a relationship, it becomes more complicated after the fact. Consequently, if you are miserable as a single person, it is highly probable that you will not be happy in a marriage. This does not mean that you will not have needs to be met by your spouse. I am saying that you should not marry to find happiness, but you should marry to share the happiness you already have. Otherwise, the unhappiness you bring from your past into your new relationship will more than likely hinder your ability to perform as a healthy unit in the *present* with your wife or husband.

Inner Pain Will Make You Bitter or Better

> It always may not be clear as to what role inner pain plays in accomplishing what God has already intended for us; but one thing is clear, inner pain will make us bitter or better.

All of our experiences may be instrumental in fulfilling God's purpose and plan in our lives. When it comes to inner pain, there is no exception. It always

The Power of Forgiveness

may not be clear as to what role inner pain plays in accomplishing what God has intended for us, but one thing is clear, inner pain will make us bitter or better.

I can recall earlier in our ministry when my husband and me experienced severe pain and hurt. One such experience came during a time when God was blessing our church tremendously, and it experienced phenomenal growth. It appeared that Satan dispatched his angels of destruction who had been given the ultimate mission to bring havoc into the body and destroy the ministry. The work had become our life and our livelihood. This was the first of one of the most painful experiences we had ever encountered as church leaders. It was a heart-throbbing ordeal. I believe what made the experience so painful was we were like some new babes in Christ. They expect no hurt and pain; they think everything is going to be wonderful when they get saved. We, at that point in our ministry, were somewhat the same way; even though we had been saved for quite a while, we had not anticipated any painful blows in the leadership arena of ministry.

I hasten to say my particular disheartening experience, at times, made me feel that something was wrong with us. I felt that perhaps we were not doing something right. The fact that we are human, I'm sure we didn't do everything right. I became skeptical and apprehensive because I anticipated attacks from certain people coming into our church. All of these emotions certainly impacted my performance. While the ministry has endured other painful encounters, I have never had another experience to affect my emotions and performance to that magnitude. Perhaps, it is because I have learned Satan's tactics, and I have matured and become better prepared to handle such conflicts.

I will forever believe this heart-throbbing experience came to build my spiritual tenacity; it also revealed my character. While I experienced pain and anger, somewhere during the course of my struggle, I came to the realization that the trial made me better instead of bitter. I became more equipped to love people, in spite of their hurting me. It put me in a position where I had to learn to trust God to keep the minds' of the people focused when the enemy had clearly attacked the ministry with a *Spirit of Distraction*. God brought us through, and we never had to fight our own battles. In fact, we could not have won had we tried.

I must admit, there were times when I wanted to take matters into my own hands, but the Holy Spirit would restrain me. I knew I had to hold my peace, and let the Lord fight my battle. I became convinced that God's ministry could not be built by fighting evil with evil. The truth is, it was too much for me. I was in the middle of the first of the most tumultuous experiences I had ever encountered in ministry. Where feelings are concerned, I felt helpless. I was hurting mainly for my husband. He was such a gentleman, who never tried to

The Power of Forgiveness

retaliate in any way to anyone. I did not know it then, but I do now, that the attack was not against us, but it was against God; it was God who had established the ministry. We sat under our pastor, the late Bishop Randolph N. Johnson and served him faithfully until his death. There were times when other leaders tried to lure us with promises of a brighter opportunity to do kingdom work, but those things did not move us. Somehow we knew we were already doing the work God had entrusted to us, and that made it great. Therefore, we stayed focused even in the midst of our hurt. *Focus* is the ability to concentrate on and continue the work God has entrusted into your hands.

The bible teaches that we are not to be overcome by evil, but to overcome evil with good; this is required, not only in our personal lives, but even when it comes to the work of the ministry. In order to overcome, there are certain guidelines I used to help me, and I will share the methodology I used later in Chapter VII. My brothers and sisters, you do not have to resolve to bitterness; you can overcome the evils of your life just as I, if you apply the balm of God's word to your hurt. You can begin your journey of inner healing by adhering to Romans 12:17-21 (NIV) which reads as follows:

Do not repay anyone evil for evil. Be careful to do what is right in the eyes of everybody.

If it is possible, as far as it depends on you, live at peace with everyone.

Do not take revenge, my friends, but leave room for God's wrath, for it is written: "It is mine to avenge; I will repay," says the Lord.

On the contrary: "If your enemy is hungry, feed him; if he is thirsty, give him something to drink. In doing this, you will heap burning coals on his head."

Do not be overcome by evil, but overcome evil with good.

As I look back over my hurt during our earlier days in ministry, I realize that those experiences were the vehicles God used to bring me to a level of maturity that would prepare me for ministry in the future. Now, I can say that when adversities befall us, God is getting ready to move us to the next level. Therefore, I view each conflict as a means of preparing us for the move. Today, I have overcome those earlier hurts by not rendering evil for evil. I do not hesitate to say that for me, it was not easy. Nevertheless, God never commands us to do anything that He has not given us the power to do. According to Philippians 2:13, the Holy Ghost works in us to help us to will and to do of our Father's good pleasure. Consequently, what the enemy designs to break us, God uses to make us. What he intends for our destruction, God uses for our perfection. Therefore, I was able to come through, not just a conqueror, but more than a conqueror through Christ Jesus who loves me.

CHAPTER IV: A REMEDY FOR INNER HEALING

🎆🎆🎆🎆🎆🎆🎆🎆🎆🎆🎆🎆🎆🎆🎆🎆🎆🎆🎆🎆🎆🎆🎆🎆🎆🎆🎆🎆
In totality, the remedy for inner healing is to simply "forgive."
🎆🎆🎆🎆🎆🎆🎆🎆🎆🎆🎆🎆🎆🎆🎆🎆🎆🎆🎆🎆🎆🎆🎆🎆🎆🎆🎆🎆

Why Forgiveness is Necessary

To forgive is a process. It is a simple word we use all the time, but to put it into practice is not quite as simple. It is easy to say, "I forgive," but many times it may not be as easy to do. Just as it takes time to become bitter, when you have been very deeply hurt, it takes time to forgive. The important thing is that you must decide to let go. When you do, God sees your heart, and as you begin to forgive, you will be able to receive forgiveness. During the course of time, you will realize that you don't feel the animosity and hatred that held you bound in the past. It is God's will that we forgive, and He helps us to do what He desires.

If you are bitter, forgive and let the hurt begin to heal. If you have been deeply hurt and feel no one loves you, as you begin to heal, you will find that there are people who truly love you, and you will be able to receive that love you have longed to have. You will come to realize that you are invaluable. You will

The Power of Forgiveness

become conscious of the fact that you are made in the image and likeness of God. This alone makes you worthy of God's love; it makes you worthy of having loving people in your life that will respect and treat you with honor. Consequently, you will begin to have a brighter outlook on life and see things from a new perspective. You will be empowered to develop wholesome relationships with family and friends, but more importantly, you will be able to develop an intimate relationship with the Almighty God. There are numerous hurting people who have not come to this point in their painful experiences. They are full of anger, bitterness, and resentment. They are not hurting just because they have been hurt, but sometimes because they resolve not to forgive.

It is not easy to forgive when you have been very deeply bruised with wounds that are life changing and personality altering; it is not as easy to let go of hurts that adversely affect how you live and where you live. For example, it may not be easy to forgive a trusted family member who molested you as a child, or parents that failed to provide you with a nurturing family environment. It is understandable if you have difficulty forgiving the spouse that walked away and left you to raise children by yourself. It may be very hard to let go when your sister, brother, or another loved one has been injured severely. It is understandable if you have difficulty forgiving someone who murdered your spouse, child, mother or father; and the list goes on. While it may not be easy, it is not impossible.

Therefore, you must forgive such hurts before you are overcome with anger, bitterness, and resentment.

Possessing the capability to forgive is powerful, and it is a godlike characteristic; when we practice it, we become empowered. It enables us to reclaim everything that was lost through harboring anger, bitterness, and resentment. Thus, we are able to recover our health. We become endowed with strength to regain our joy and peace. Forgiveness provides the power to rescue broken fellowships and relationships. More importantly, it empowers us to love God and to express it one toward another by the Holy Ghost that is spread abroad in our hearts. In totality, the remedy for inner healing is to simply "forgive." Forgiveness has mind-changing, heart-transforming, and life-revolutionizing power. It has the power to make you better and not bitter. It has the power to enable you to become what God has intended for you to be, and it equips you to do what God has planned for your life.

༄༄༄༄༄༄༄༄༄༄༄༄༄༄༄༄༄༄༄༄༄༄༄༄༄༄༄༄
However, when the human is empowered by the divine, all things become possible.
༄༄༄༄༄༄༄༄༄༄༄༄༄༄༄༄༄༄༄༄༄༄༄༄༄༄༄༄

The ability to forgive is a divine attribute; it is too hard to accomplish through human abilities. However, when the human is empowered by the divine, all things become possible. God's love is so strong that He enters into our situations. He helps us to want to do His will,

The Power of Forgiveness

and not only so, but He empowers us to do it. It is God's good pleasure to see His children forgive and be forgiven, to forgive and be healed. We are told in Philippians 2:13 (NIV):

For it is God who works in you to will and to act according to his good purpose.

Since God is working in us to help us do what He has purposed, we can be assured that He will empower us to forgive. Jesus clearly lets us know if we want to be forgiven, we must forgive others. Above all, remember that God will give you the power you need to forgive and receive the benefits of forgiveness.

A Revelation Unfolds

Jesus gives the following command in Mark 11:25-26:

And when ye stand praying, forgive, if ye have ought against any: that your Father also which is in heaven may forgive you your trespasses.

But if ye do not forgive, neither will your Father which is in heaven forgive your trespasses.

Naturally if we are holding something in our hearts against someone, we must let it go. Much emotional healing is experienced as we forgive. Harboring unforgiveness is a sin, and when we are guilty, our emotional healing is hindered. First, we cannot receive it because God does not hear our prayers, and secondly, He does not accept our sacrifice of worship.

For years, I had read right over these powerful verses found in Mark 11:25-26. On one occasion, as I read this passage, I began to receive a revelation to forgiveness. The words sprang up from the pages of the bible as the message began to unfold. I was overwhelmed with this new enlightenment. My heart felt as though it had begun to beat with twice the frequency. As I read this scripture, for the first time, I was able to understand why some people battle with their inner hurt and pain for years. The revelation of this scripture held the key to the present performance of many deeply wounded people. The agony of their heartache is so torturing that it paralyzes and inhibits their ability to effectively do kingdom work; in many instances, they need inner healing. However, they cannot receive it until they embrace a heart to forgive.

Unforgiveness is the key to many inner hurts, and forgiveness unlocks the doorway to much inner healing. This insight was extremely different from what I was accustomed to hearing, and it was very hard for me to accept. It was difficult for me because as an adolescent growing up in the church, I had seen so much bitterness amongst the body of believers, and as an adult, I continued to witness it. However, of greater significance to me was the startling reality that I too had personal issues with forgiveness. I, being the person

The Power of Forgiveness

that I am, invest much of myself into others. When those to whom I have given much of my time, my energy, and myself wound me, I find it very difficult to forgive. More profoundly, the revelation of the power of forgiveness has been a mind-changing, heart-transforming, and life-revolutionizing experience for me.

The devil knows the power of forgiveness, and he also knows the impact of unforgiveness. His plans are to keep you in darkness and feeling sorry for yourself. As long as you are engaged in a *pity party,* you are going to have problems forgiving. The bad thing about a *pity party* is the devil convinces you that you are really okay because you just feel hurt. You are not bitter, nor resentful—just hurt. Nevertheless, any kind of pain, physical or emotional that continues to hurt, is a sign of a problem. Thus, if emotional pain continues, chances are, it eventually will evolve into emotional bitterness. When one becomes bitter, he will suffer more tremendous inner hurt. Pain of this magnitude not only damages one emotionally, but it takes a physical and spiritual toll on its victims as well. Hence, the sin of unforgiveness at work in the life of a believer can inhibit him from becoming all he was meant to be.

What It Means to Forgive and Forget

It is imperative to realize that as long as we embrace our hurts, we become candidates for harboring unforgiveness. I am not implying that deep wounds do not leave scars, but normally, scars don't hurt. Scars are merely reminders of our experiences. When we receive inner healing, the scars never dictate our judgment relative to our offenders. This is what it means to "forgive and forget." I Thessalonians 5:15 reads as follows:

See that none render evil for evil unto any man; but ever follow that which is good, both among yourselves, and to all men.

This verse commands us to seek to do right toward those who treat us right and also to those who mistreat us. In essence it means, do right by all people; here "all" includes those who hurt us as well. To forget does not mean that we lose our mental capacity to remember that we have been wounded, nor does it mean that we cannot remember who offended us. Forget in the sense of forgiveness means that we do not take advantage of an opportunity to repay evil for evil. While you may be very aware that someone has harmed you, you must seek to do right by him even when you have an opportunity to get revenge.

To forgive a person does not imply that you must continue an ongoing physical relationship with him; also, it does not mean that a person who violates the laws of the land should not be held accountable for his actions. It would be foolish to continue to give a person access to your house if you learned he was using it for an unlawful activity. While you may love the person

The Power of Forgiveness

dearly, his character trait would dictate that he was not trustworthy. The fact that you could not trust him would alter the type of relationship you may have had in the past. Nevertheless, when you forgive a person, you would not take advantage of an opportunity to overcome evil by doing wrong.

For example, I am reminded of a person who had a fall on some property we owned. A couple of months later, we received a statement indicating that this person wanted two hundred dollars to assist with some doctor bills. This was the first time we had been informed that a doctor had treated the person relative to the fall. In the statement, it was clear that we would be sued if we did not pay the requested two hundred dollars. We had no problem paying the bill, but we were concerned about many of the surrounding circumstances. However, my husband discreetly took care of the matter.

As fate would have it, this person ended up at our mercy. Here was an opportunity to render evil for evil. We had not mentally forgotten about what had happened earlier; we just did not take it into account. This person's past behavior did not dictate our decision. Therefore, to forgive means to let go, and when you let something go, for all practical reasons, you forget it. When you forget it, you write it off. This is what God does when He forgives us for our sins. He writes them off of our account. The devil will look for them, but he will not be able to find them. He will not be able to find our sins because what God forgets, He expunges—they are never, ever brought up again. God has not and never will impute what He has forgiven. He separates our sins from us as far as the East is from the West. Psalms 103:12 reads:

As far as the east is from the west, so far hath he removed our transgressions from us.

Jeremiah 31:34 reads as follows:

...Saith the Lord: for I will forgive their iniquity, and I will remember their sin no more.

For God to never remember our sin means that he will not recall them in the judgment. The wonderful thing about the power of forgiveness is that God treats us as though we never committed the offense. When we forgive, we will do the same.

Consequently, we are not required to mentally forget the hurt that someone may have caused us, but we are required not to take an account of it. Presently, if we are mentally forgetting all of the pain people caused us, eventually, we are not going to remember any of the joys they bring. The power of forgiveness is demonstrated when we are aware that someone has hurt us, and yet we are able to function in a given situation as if it had never happened.

The Power of Forgiveness

Nevertheless, if we are to mentally forget the pain someone inflicted upon us, how could we ever give a testimony of the victories in our lives? If we could not think back on our agonizing hurts, we would never have an occasion to make a decision to do right toward those who despitefully used us. Also, if we could have no recollection of those who cursed us, how would we be able to choose to pray for them as we are commanded to do in Luke 6:28? Correspondingly, when we fully let go, we will be able to function accordingly, and the ability to recall our hurtful experiences will become vital in our ministry. As I discussed in Chapter III, this is what made Joseph's treatment of his brothers with kindness so powerful. He did not mentally forget what they had done to him; also, he did not use it to get revenge when it was in his power to do so; to operate at that level is a divine characteristic. It is not impossible, but divine. It is not something we can do of ourselves. It takes the power of God at work around us and within us to move to this spiritual plateau.

Until we come to a point where we are able to minister in this manner, there is a possibility that we need to forgive. It is understandable that it is not always easy to get to this point. Some ills are more difficult to reconcile than others. Nevertheless, when we harbor unforgiveness, it will grip us until we become bitter; when this happens, we cannot win. Ultimately, as a result of unforgiveness, we will be victimized twice, once by the hurt inflicted upon us by another and again by our own actions.

Martha L. Crockett

Grace Helps Us to Forgive the Unforgivable

With the knowledge that harboring unforgiveness is a direct transgression against God's law, I cannot over emphasize the importance of forgiveness in the life of a believer. The fact is, while we may appear to be making progress, we cannot really move forward until we forgive. Forgiveness is too difficult to accomplish merely by human will. Therefore, God has provided a means that enables us to let go of what may be viewed as the unforgivable hurt. The only unforgivable sin the bible addresses is to blaspheme against the Holy Ghost. Consequently, whatever offense someone commits against us is forgivable. It is when someone commits what appears to be the unforgivable that we need more than human strength. Since we cannot do this on our own, we need the grace of God to help us to do what we cannot humanly accomplish.

The sufficiency of God's grace enables us to fulfill impossible missions. *Grace* is a free gift of God. It is an unmerited favor. We cannot do enough to earn it. God decides to bestow it upon us. If we had access to all the riches of this world and the world to come, we could not purchase grace. By the grace of God, we can obtain the help we need to do what He commands us to do. As I stated earlier, God commands us to forgive before we can receive forgiveness. Apart from God, we can do nothing. Nevertheless, we can do all things through His strength. We receive His strength through the gift of the *Holy Spirit.* If you do not have the Spirit abiding in your life, pause at this time and sincerely ask God to come into your soul and save you. Ask him to empower you to forgive and to be healed. The key to inner healing is the power to forgive. The power to forgive requires divine help to achieve. However, if we do not have God in us, we are already fighting a loosing battle. Inner pain is of an emotional nature that affects our spiritual self; Hence, the healing for inner hurt is of a spiritual significance. No human strength is powerful enough to win a spiritual battle; it is a job for God. II Corinthians 10:3-6 addresses spiritual warfare in the following manner:

For though we walk in the flesh, we do not war after the flesh:

(For the weapons of our warfare are not carnal, but mighty through God to the pulling down of strong holds;)

Casting down imaginations, and every high thing that exalteth itself against the knowledge of God, and bringing into captivity every thought to the obedience of Christ;

And having in a readiness to revenge all disobedience, when your obedience is fulfilled.

Even after we have been born of God, at times, we will still experience hurt that will appear to be impossible to bear. We will also need reassurance that God makes things work together for the good of those who love Him.

The Danger of Walking in Unforgiveness

There is a danger of walking in *unforgiveness*. To walk in unforgiveness is to hold on to hurt and pain and to refuse to release others of the sins that they committed against us. It may cause us to lose touch with our real feelings. When this happens, we have a tendency to forget what really caused our hurt. Even worse, it causes us to harbor anger, bitterness, and resentment. We may appear to be effective in building the kingdom of God, but we are not effective in God. This is one reason why many will profess what wonderful works they have done, but God will tell them to depart from Him because He never knew them. Matthew 7:21-23 (NIV) reads as follows:

"Not everyone who says to me, 'Lord, Lord,' will enter the kingdom of heaven, but only he who does the will of my Father who is in heaven.

Many will say to me on that day, 'Lord, Lord, did we not prophesy in your name, and in your name drive out demons and perform many miracles?'

Then I will tell them plainly, 'I never knew you. Away from me, you evildoers!'..."

There are people who are able to do great and mighty kingdom work, and yet stand before God in condemnation. The scripture never declared that God said that they did not do the wonderful works, but He did say He never knew them. Their works were wonderful, but their labor was in vain. *Work* is your assignment or mission upon this earth; *labor* is the energy and strength you expend to accomplish your mission. Hence, it is possible to run a race and yet not win the prize. In like manner, we can do God's work without the favor of God, and yet not enter into eternal life. Actually, we can bring many souls into the kingdom and miss the mark ourselves. I Corinthians 9:19-27(NIV) reads as follows:

Though I am free and belong to no man, I make myself a slave to everyone, to win as many as possible.

To the Jews I became like a Jew, to win the Jews. To those under the law I became like one under the law (though I myself am not under the law), so as to win those under the law.

To those not having the law I became like one not having the law (though I am not free from God's law but am under Christ's law), so as to win those not having the law.

To the weak I became weak, to win the weak. I have become all things to all men so that by all possible means I might save some.

I do all this for the sake of the gospel, that I may share in its blessings.

Do you not know that in a race all the runners run, but only one gets the prize? Run in such a way as to get the prize.

Everyone who competes in the games goes into strict training. They do it to get a crown that will not last; but we do it to get a crown that will last forever.

Therefore I do not run like a man running aimlessly; I do not fight like a man beating the air.

No, I beat my body and make it my slave so that after I have preached to others, I myself will not be disqualified for the prize.

There are other sins that will cause people to be condemned when they stand before God. Nevertheless, it is clear that the sin of unforgiveness, which is mentioned earlier in Mark 11:25-26 will cause God not to accept our worship; neither, does he forgive us for our sins when we do not forgive those who sin against us. Now let's go back and look at Mark. 11:25-26 where it reads:

And when ye stand praying, forgive, if ye have ought against any; that your Father also which is in heaven may forgive you your trespasses.

But if ye do not forgive, neither will your Father which is in heaven forgive your trespasses.

Prayer is a form of worship; the word of God admonished that when we stand praying to forgive if we have an ought against anyone. Matt 5:23-24 reads as follows:

Therefore if thou bring thy gift to the altar, and there rememberest that thy brother hath ought against thee;

Leave there thy gift before the altar, and go thy way; first be reconciled to thy brother, and then come and offer thy gift.

God commands us to be reconciled with our brothers and then to come and offer our gifts. If we do not follow God's directions for worship, He will not accept our gift as God will not receive our sacrifice when we offer it in disobedience. God did not accept Saul's sacrifice when he disobeyed His orders. Samuel told Saul in I Samuel 15:22, that it is better to obey than to sacrifice.

When we come before God to worship, it is absolutely necessary that we forgive; it is of utmost importance that we be reconciled with our brothers. After we have been reconciled, then we may offer our gift. Why is it important that we follow this order? First of all, God commands us to do it, and secondly, Mark 11:25-26 clearly states that if we do not forgive the trespasses of others, neither will our Heavenly Father forgive our trespasses. A good thing about forgiving is that as you forgive you will be forgiven.

The model prayer in Matthews 6:12 reads on this order:

"Forgive us our debts as we forgive our debtors."

Our Heavenly Father chooses to forgive us as we forgive those who trespass against us. I have often heard it said that harboring anger, bitterness, and resentment has a tendency to accelerate the aging process, and can cause high blood pressure, diabetes, cancer, and other related diseases; all of which, can lead to a premature death. If, peradventure, this is medically and scientifically true, it behooves all of us to beware of the sin of unforgiveness. We were not created to carry the load unforgiveness brings. We were created to glorify God in our mortal bodies and in our spirits.

The Power of Forgiveness

We will be unable to glorify God in our bodies and minds while succumbing under the load of anger, bitterness, and resentment. What we can do when we go before God in this state is offer Him our contrite spirit. We must confess our feelings, and ask Him to help us to let go of our hurt. God is just; He knows we need time to get over our inner pain. He does not write us off when we hurt. Neither will He accept our sacrifice when we cover our sins. When we cover our sins of unforgiveness, God does not accept anything but repentance. The bible lets us know when we cover our sins we cannot prosper. Proverbs 28:13:

He that covereth his sins shall not prosper: but whoso confesseth and forsaketh them shall have mercy.

The problem with unforgiveness is that we carry the burden of all the sins we commit subsequently not to forgiving those who sin against us. We carry these burdens because when we do not forgive, God does not forgive our sins. Some may question His order of forgiveness. God is Sovereign. He can do what He wants, when He wants and how He wants; He is right because He is God.

※※※※※※※※※※※※※※※※※※※※※※※※※※※※※※※
The problem with unforgiveness is that we carry the burden of all the sins we commit subsequently not to forgiving those who sin against us.
※※※※※※※※※※※※※※※※※※※※※※※※※※※※※※※

CHAPTER V: CHANNELS OF BLESSINGS AND CURSES

In Exodus 15:26, God spoke to the children of Israel and said:

...If thou wilt diligently hearken to the voice of the LORD thy God, and wilt do that which is right in his sight, and wilt give ear to his commandments, and keep all his statutes, I will put none of these diseases upon thee, which I have brought upon the Egyptians: for I am the LORD that healeth thee.

In this passage, God told the Israelites that He was their Healer. Also, He specifically directed them to obey His commandments. Furthermore, the Lord told them if they would hearken diligently to His voice and live righteously in His sight, He would not put any of the diseases upon them that He had brought upon the Egyptians. Hence, obedience is a channel through which the blessings of God can flow, but disobedience is a pathway for curses.

Obedience is to adhere to the word of the Lord. This text is not implying that every sickness or misfortune is a result of disobedience. However, there is a positive correlation between obedience and blessings, and disobedience and curses. Additionally,

The Power of Forgiveness

there is scriptural evidence that every sickness is not a curse per se, but a means to some other end. Sometimes, sickness and other unfavorable circumstances are instruments by which we are brought into a place to learn invaluable life lessons. It could be a test by divine permission, such as in the case of Job as referenced in Chapter III. It could be a means to an end to help us understand where others are. The capacity to participate in the feelings of others is *empathy,* and some people have to actually experience what others experience in order to understand what others feel. There are some who cannot exercise empathy without the benefit of actually sitting in others' seats and walking in their shoes. For example, some people don't seem to be able to empathize with people, who are sick, until they become sick themselves. There are other people who are unable to empathize with people who are experiencing inner anguish, until they have had a personal encounter.

The ability to express empathy empowers us to minister to people in a personal way. It is a characteristic of Christ. It enables us to become involved in another's situation as if it were our own. Without empathy, it is difficult to minister effectively. If we do not possess this gift, it is impossible to fulfill the law of Christ, Galatians 6:2 reads:

Bear ye one another's burdens, and so fulfil the law of Christ.

The law of Christ is love. When we have love one for another, we exemplify true Christianity. Jesus not only wants us to say we have love, but he wants us to demonstrate it. It is what lets the world know that we are truly followers of Christ. Jesus makes this clear in John 13:34-35:

A new commandment I give unto you, That ye love one another; as I have loved you, that ye also love one another.

By this shall all men know that ye are my disciples, if ye have love one to another.

Consequently, every agonizing encounter or sickness is not a curse for the sake of a curse, but can serve as a means to a better end. One thing is clear, God promises to bless those who are obedient, and those who are disobedient will be cursed. When we are obedient, and unfortunate things happen to us, we must trust God to work in the midst of our adversities. Trust Him to bring a blessing out of what appears to be a curse. The bible lets us know in Romans 8:28 that all things work together for the good of them that love God and are called for His purpose.

Even in the midst of our painful circumstances, we must remember that obedience is a channel through which our blessings flow. Therefore, good physical and emotional health may come as a result of observing God's law. To adhere to the words of the Lord brings about wholeness in the life of a believer and a meaningful relationship with others and ultimately, with God.

The blessings that come by taking heed to the decrees of the Almighty are further emphasized in the 28th chapter of Deuteronomy. It admonishes that blessings will be commanded to come upon those who are obedient to God. The scripture speaks of blessings upon their bodies, posterity, and properties. The flip side to this is that curses may come as a result of disobedience, and those who refuse to adhere to God's commandments may be overcome with sorrow. Their bodies will be cursed; their children will be cursed; their land will be cursed, and they will not prosper.

Again in Exodus 15:22-26, we see where Moses led the children of Israel from the Red Sea. They wandered in the wilderness of Shur for three days and found no water. Finally, they came to the waters of Marah. They could not drink thereof because the waters were bitter. The people murmured against Moses, and he cried unto the Lord. The Lord showed him a tree, and when Moses cast it into the waters, they were made sweet. It was at the waters of Marah that God made a statue and an ordinance for the people and put them to a test. At this place where the waters were bitter, God revealed Himself as the great Jehovah-Raphe, the God that heals. He promised that He would put none of the diseases upon them that He had brought upon the Egyptians if they would only obey.

Disobedience ties God's hands; it is the transgressing of God's law, and it holds up blessings of healing and deliverance. While God yearns to see His children complete, He cannot make them whole where there is disobedience. To disregard and disobey His commandments is a sure way to invite curses upon the life of the transgressor. Let's keep in mind, obedience to God is one of the best means by which we have access to a healthy and fulfilled life.

CHAPTER VI: ANGER IS DANGEROUS

The Importance of Mastering Anger

Anger is a state of displeasure with an attitude to get revenge. When we have been hurt and do not control our emotions, it will more than likely evolve into anger. One of the best ways to manage anger is to deal with hurts and pains as soon as possible. There is a story of Cain, the oldest son of Adam and Eve, in the fourth chapter of Genesis that reveals what can happen when we fail to master anger. The bible lets us know that Abel tended the sheep, and Cain tilled the ground. During the process of time, Abel brought of the firstling and the fat thereof to offer unto God. God had respect for Abel and his offering. Cain brought of the fruit of the ground, and offered it to God. God did not respect Cain and his offering; Cain became angry.

It is important to note that the problem was not the nature of the gift, but it was the attitude of the giver. As a result of Cain's anger, the Lord spoke to him and asked why was he so angry and cast down. God told him that if he would do right, his gift would be accepted; He also cautioned him, if he did not do what was right, sin would be crouched at his door. He made Cain very aware that sin desired to control him.

God also made him conscious that he needed to master sin, or it would master him.

Martha L. Crockett

God is so good; He gives us time to deal with our pains and hurts. His talking to Cain provided an opportunity for Cain to deal with his. Cain chose not to let go; he chose to continue to be jealous and angry with his brother. He became deceitful and fooled Abel into the field, and slew him. His choice to continue in anger drove him to become a pioneer of murder. Even though his behavior caused Abel's death; ultimately, he hurt himself. He was driven from his family; he was driven from his homeland; he was driven from the face of God; he became a wanderer in the earth. The earth that had brought forth fruit in abundance for him would no longer yield her strength. Cain, himself, declared that his punishment was greater than he could bear. His choice not to deal with his anger caused him to become a broken and miserable person. Not only was his uncontrolled anger destructive to others; consequently, it became destructive to him.

How To Manage Anger

Ephesians 4:26-37 provides insight for dealing with anger. We are instructed to be angry and not sin, nor to let the sun go down on our wrath. Also, we are warned not to give space to the devil. When we fail to resolve anger, it gives the devil an open door to our inner self, and all kinds of ugly feelings will dominate.

When we become driven by ugly feelings, we can expect various kinds of emotional ills such as anger, bitterness, and resentment to dictate our behavior. This is all the more reason that when you are in the midst of your most trying situation, remember to keep in mind the words of God to Cain in Genesis 4:7 (NIV):

If you do what is right, will you not be accepted? But if you do not do what is right, sin is crouching at your door; it desires to have you, but you must master it.

One of the best ways to master anger is to let it go. It is important to understand that to be angry is not a sin, but to continue to be angry until we become bitter is. To be angry is a human emotion. It is divine also; God becomes angry. Therefore, He knows how important it is to deal with anger before it ends in total destruction. However, God's anger cannot be destructive toward Himself. It will only destroy its objects. God is perfect, and His anger is perfect. He knows that His anger will never cause Him pain. He also, knows how devastating it can be upon its object, and therefore, He tells us in Isaiah 54:7-8:

For a small moment have I forsaken thee; but with great mercies will I gather thee.

In a little wrath I hid my face from thee for a moment; but with everlasting kindness will I have mercy on thee, saith the LORD thy Redeemer.

By man's standards, a moment is a small fraction of time. For God to be angry for a moment does not have to be a moment as we know it. God knows time in a dimension we could never know. A day could be a thousand years, and a thousand years as one day according to II Peter 3:8. At any rate, we must deal with our anger before we are overcome with it. God is a loving and just Father; He provides us with time to be angry, but in all of His love and justice, He does not make provision for us to be bitter. The main thing we need to learn is that God, in His divinity, takes time, which is referred to as a small moment, to manage His anger. Therefore, we must manage ours also.

※※※※※※※※※※※※※※※※※※※※※※※※※※※※※※

God is a loving and just Father; He provides us with time to be angry, but in all of His love and justice, He does not make provision for us to be bitter.

※※※※※※※※※※※※※※※※※※※※※※※※※※※※※※

The Impact of God's Anger

Other accounts of how God deals with His anger are found in Psalms 103:8-9 and Psalms 145:8. A small moment of God's anger can totally wipe out an individual, a community, a nation, or even the entire universe. To further explore the devastating impact of God's anger, let's observe an experience of King David and the people of Israel in II Samuel the 24th chapter

The Power of Forgiveness

where God became angry with Israel. The devastation of the occurrence is found in II Samuel 24:10-25:

And David's heart smote him after that he had numbered the people. And David said unto the LORD, I have sinned greatly in that I have done: and now, I beseech thee, O LORD, take away the iniquity of thy servant; for I have done very foolishly.

For when David was up in the morning, the word of the LORD came unto the prophet Gad, David's seer, saying,

Go and say unto David, Thus saith the LORD, I offer thee three things; choose thee one of them, that I may do it unto thee.

So Gad came to David, and told him, and said unto him, Shall seven years of famine come unto thee in thy land? or wilt thou flee three months before thine enemies, while they pursue thee? or that there be three days' pestilence in thy land? Now advise, and see what answer I shall return to him that sent me.

And David said unto Gad, I am in a great strait: let us fall now into the hand of the LORD; for his mercies are great: and let me not fall into the hand of man.

So the LORD sent a pestilence upon Israel from the morning even to the time appointed: and there died of the people from Dan even to Beersheba seventy thousand men.

And when the angel stretched out his hand upon Jerusalem to destroy it, the LORD repented him of the evil, and said to the angel that destroyed the people, It is enough: stay now thine hand. And the angel of the LORD was by the threshingplace of Araunah the Jebusite.

And David spake unto the LORD when he saw the angel that smote the people, and said, Lo, I have sinned, and I have done wickedly: but these sheep, what have they done? let thine hand, I pray thee, be against me, and against my father's house.

And Gad came that day to David, and said unto him, Go up, rear an altar unto the LORD in the threshingfloor of Araunah the Jebusite.

And David, according to the saying of Gad, went up as the LORD commanded.

And Araunah looked, and saw the king and his servants coming on toward him: and Araunah went out, and bowed himself before the king on his face upon the ground.

The Power of Forgiveness

And Araunah said, Wherefore is my lord the king come to his servant? And David said, To buy the threshingfloor of thee, to build an altar unto the LORD, that the plague may be stayed from the people.

And Araunah said unto David, Let my lord the king take and offer up what seemeth good unto him: behold, here be oxen for burnt sacrifice, and threshing instruments and other instruments of the oxen for wood.

All these things did Araunah, as a king, give unto the king. And Araunah said unto the king, The LORD thy God accept thee.

And the king said unto Araunah, Nay; but Twill surely buy it of thee at a price: neither-will I offer burnt offerings unto the LORD my God of that which doth cost me nothing. So David bought the threshingfloor and the oxen for fifty shekels of silver.

And David built there an altar unto the LORD, and offered burnt offerings and peace offerings. So the LORD was entreated for the land, and the plague was stayed from Israel.

These fifteen verses provide a dramatic account of the effect that God's anger has on the object of His anger. They also provide insight into the mercy and forgiveness of God. If God were not the forgiving Father that He is, no one would be able to survive His anger, even for a short moment. These verses, also, help us to see why it is absolutely imperative that we forgive. We must forgive so that we can receive the forgiveness of God. The weight of our own sins that are not forgiven is too heavy for us to bear. Imagine what would have happened to Israel if God had not accepted David's sacrifice of repentance. Yet look at the lives that were destroyed in a short moment of God's anger. Seventy thousand men died at the hand of the angel.

Upon David's repentance, the magnitude of God's compassion and His propensity to forgive was revealed; He commanded the angel to stop destroying the people. If we want to receive forgiveness, we must repent; it does not matter what the sin is; it could be adultery, anger, hatred, or murder. *Repent* means to become sorrowful of your sins and turn away from them. In like manner, if we are to be free of our own sins, we must let go of anger before bitterness evolves. Where there is bitterness, all kinds of emotional ills will control our actions. The finished work of ill emotions will cause even more damage and inner pain. We have only two choices, to forgive and master anger, or not forgive and become overwhelmed with emotional hurt. When we hold on to our anger and don't forgive, we walk contrary to God, and when we walk contrary to Him, He walks contrary to us. Leviticus 26: 23-24

...And if ye will not be reformed by me by these things, but will walk contrary unto me;

Then will I also walk contrary unto you, and will punish you yet seven times for your sins.

Consequently, when we walk in anger toward others, it stirs the divine anger of God toward us. The impact of His anger is so destructive; we can not afford to continue to embrace the sin of our own anger by refusing to forgive. Ultimately, it is not what someone does to us that brings the destruction, but more often how we respond to it.

CHAPTER VII: A CRITICAL ANALYSIS TO INNER HEALING

> In order to get the proper perspective on the source of your hurt, you must determine if your pain caused your experiences or if your experiences caused your pain.

It is not my intent to lead anyone to believe that I have an instant four-step plan that will guarantee inner healing. However, there are four steps that will provide a means to critically analyze each situation and assist with the healing process. Because these activities were critical in my quest for deliverance from emotional hurt during my times of extreme pain, I believe they will help others who are hurting as well. One of the best ways to analyze your particular situation is by utilizing the problem solving approach. The primary activities that will aid in critically analyzing a given case are as following: (1) Determine if you are hurting, (2) Determine what caused the hurt (3) Determine your alternatives, and (4) Implement your choice.

(1) Determine That You Are Hurting

Unless God miraculously heals, there are certain procedures that must be considered for inner healing.

The Power of Forgiveness

First, one must realize that he is hurting. There are keys to help in this process. For example, there are bad, ugly, or nasty emotions that will help to identify if there is inner hurt. It may not always be clear as to exactly what they are, but when an encounter with certain people, words, pictures, or places causes emotional unrest, it will be evident that something is wrong. Such feelings include, but are not limited to, unforgiveness, anger, bitterness, hatred, resentment, and low self-esteem.

Unforgiveness is the result of holding on to pains and ills. It has to do with not letting go of hurts. It causes a person to hold grudges against another who has harmed him. When he sees the offender, there is something that makes him want to get revenge. This is a normal human reaction when there has been deep inner hurt; nonetheless, there comes a time when one must forgive.

Anger is another ugly feeling. It is displeasure with an attitude to get revenge. A person full of anger may want his offender to hurt, just as the offender hurt him. According to Vine's Expository Dictionary of Old and New Testament Words, by W.E. Vine, anger implies a lingering condition. Anger that is not appeased during the process of time will evolve into bitterness.

Bitterness leads to more serious complications. Bitterness is a harsh and strong feeling that develops as the result of ongoing anger. It is a piercing and painful experience. It may tremendously affect health and emotions. Some of its characteristics are hatred and resentment.

Hatred is a passionate dislike for someone. When one hates a person, he wishes all kinds of evil upon him. He wishes the person was dead or that something very bad would happen to him. He may literally become sick when he sees the person.

Resentment works on the emotions as well. The Webster's New Collegiate Dictionary states that resentment is a persistent ill feeling. When one is resentful toward a person, it causes him to be easily annoyed by his or her presence. It causes exceptional sensitiveness and arouses responses.

Low self-esteem is a very painful feeling. Evident of its presence is to feel very bad about one's self; one feels worthless. He does not like himself, and therefore, feels that no one else likes him. Low self-esteem can make a person who is very gorgeous physically feel very unattractive. It can also make some people act as though they think more highly of themselves than they really do. Some may put others down to make themselves feel better. It may drive them to get involved in activities that can be detrimental to their health. They may become sexually promiscuous or perverted; they may become an alcoholic, a drug abuser, a habitual overeater, a murderer, and such. Actually, anger, hatred, bitterness, resentment, and low self-esteem are emotional ills that can gain strongholds over people who harbor unforgiveness.

(2) Determine What Caused the Hurt

Upon the realization of your hurt, you must recognize its cause. The cause may be a result of present or past experiences, such as verbal or physical abuse. As you experience verbal or physical abuse from someone, you may have problems relating to the people in your classroom, on your job, or in the church, and the like. In order to get the proper perspective on the source of your hurt, you must determine if your pain caused your experiences or if your experiences caused your pain. If the first is true, then the related problems are merely symptoms of your inner hurts. The same is true for past hurts. Sometimes, focusing on the symptoms of inner wounds for an extended period may cause one to become confused as to when and where the inner pain began. Therefore, isolate the source of your pain. It is detrimental to focus on symptoms because they change and can become even more complicated, but the initial source of pain remains constant.

(3) Determine Your Alternatives and Select Your Best Choice

Once you recognize that you are hurting and identify the cause of your hurt, you are ready to move to the third step. In this step, you must determine your options; there are at least two. (l)You must accept that you are hurting and resolve to let it go, or (2) you may choose to continue to hurt. It would be unwise to select the second option. Therefore, while generally believing in the healing power of God, there has to be an acceptance of His will for deliverance from your particular hurt. Also, you must decide to let go of your pain. Acceptance here does not imply that you resolve to continue hurting, but it is a leap of faith in that you acknowledge your hurt, and you come to a decision to let it go. In order to receive inner healing, it is imperative to know that you have a need to be healed. Equally as important, you must embrace the delivering power of God, and apply the ointment of His word to your pain. John 8:32 and 36 read as follows:

And ye shall know the truth, and the truth shall make you free.

If the Son therefore shall make you free, ye shall be free indeed.

If you don't know and neither accept that you are hurting, you deprive yourself of the freedom that comes from knowing the truth. No matter how painful your wounds are, you must face the reality of their presence. While facing your pain, there is comfort in knowing that God's word provides inner healing for your deep hurts. Knowing and accepting that Jesus loves and died for you are a move toward your freedom in Christ.

The Power of Forgiveness

When Jesus makes you free, you are completely liberated, and become empowered to begin applying the healing balm of God's word.

(4) Prayerfully Implement Your Choice

Prayer is a powerful antidote for inner healing. Therefore, it is not enough to know that there is healing for the hurting, but you must implement what you know through prayer. In other words, you must apply God's word to your hurt by becoming engulfed in what He has said. In essence, God's word is a means of healing; it helps you to get to the other side of your pain. Psalms 107:20 reveals that God sent his word and healed them. God's word is full of healing power for every situation.

Sometimes your hurt may be so painful that you may need to pray and fast. When *fasting,* you do not eat and sometimes you don't intake liquids along with prayer. Fasting works wonders for your spiritual and physical self. Jesus tells his disciples that some things come forth by nothing but prayer and fasting. Mark 9:29 reads as follows:

And he said unto them, This kind can come forth by nothing, but by prayer and fasting.

CHAPTER VIII: THE HEALING POWER OF A DISCIPLINED PRAYER LIFE

🎟🎟🎟🎟🎟🎟🎟🎟🎟🎟🎟🎟🎟🎟🎟🎟🎟🎟🎟🎟🎟🎟🎟🎟🎟🎟🎟🎟🎟
A life that lacks self-control is out of control.
🎟🎟🎟🎟🎟🎟🎟🎟🎟🎟🎟🎟🎟🎟🎟🎟🎟🎟🎟🎟🎟🎟🎟🎟🎟🎟🎟🎟🎟

Prayer is talking with God and waiting for God to talk back to us. When we talk to Him, we come to know Him as a personal friend. It is a powerful weapon God has given to the believer. It is a core instrument, which is to be used in our spiritual warfare. It empowers to quench all the fiery darts of the devil and to pull down strongholds. A Christian must practice prayer in order to be effective in carrying out his divine assignment. Also, he must possess certain virtues to develop an effective prayer life. A major key for applying God's word through prayer for inner hurts is discipline. *Discipline* is synonymous with self-control. It is an attribute of the fruit of the Spirit. It is referred to as temperance in the King James Version. We have to exercise temperance in order to stick to a fitness program. We need it in order to stay on our jobs. It is necessary to reach our goals and to realize our dreams. It is of utmost importance to assert discipline in every area of our lives. A life that lacks self-control is out of control.

The Power of Forgiveness

Just like we need temperance in monitoring and maintaining our secular activities, we need it to exercise good moral and spiritual habits. We need self-discipline to develop a prayer life. Actually, prayer helps us to be disciplined, and discipline helps us to pray. It is in prayer where we develop a wholesome relationship with our Maker. When we have a good relationship with God, we are able to access what He already has ordained for us before the foundation of the world. As a result, we become endowed with extraordinary abilities to grasp great and marvelous things. Praying impregnates us with the power of God to receive great revelations and unusual strength emerges.

Talking with God helps us to gained strength to do things that are humanly impossible. Through prayer, I have been empowered with unprecedented courage at a time when it was most needed. The time I spent talking with God was when I received some of my greatest insights.

For instance, I had often heard people testify, "I will let nothing separate me from the love of God." Since they would reference Romans 8:35, I embraced this testimony just as I heard it. I too felt, I would let nothing separate me from the love of God. I recall one morning while in prayer and meditation; I began to read Romans chapter eight. As I read Romans 8:35-39, a new enlightenment embraced my spirit. It appeared as though I was reading something other than what I had been reading. I became excited as I began to see that *human will* is not powerful enough to keep us from being separated from the love of God. Also, *human will* is not powerful enough to keep us in God's love. It is all God's doing. Not that our love is so strong toward Him, but His is so strong toward us. In fact, God's love is so strong that nothing, absolutely nothing, can separate us from Him. Even Satan himself cannot pluck us out of His hands. Yes! Great revelations come through prayer. Therefore, we must make prayer a lifestyle, and it comes through temperance. Without self-control, we cannot develop a prayer life. Without discipline, we will not be able to exercise the spiritual habits that are necessary for our inner healing.

CHAPTER IX: THE HEALING POWER OF THE WORD AND THE BLOOD

The Healing Power of God's Word

The Psalmist tells us that God sent His word and delivered them. Truly there is enough deliverance in the word of God to turn your darkest midnight into day. Nevertheless, the word cannot deliver you until you apply it to your pain. For example, I recall the night when my mother's approaching death became a reality to me. She had been severely suffering with cancer for three months. I had spent almost every day driving from my hometown of Petersburg to the hospital where she was in Richmond, Virginia. I found myself engulfed in tears as I drove up the highway. I was crying and hurt because I hated to see her endure so much suffering. However, at no time during the first 2½ months did I imagine my mother would not survive a very critical operation. Nevertheless, when I perceived the inevitable, my emotions took on another dimension. Not only did I experience emotional hurt, but also, my heart became gripped with fear.

Certainly, the mother I had known for thirty-seven years could not be dying. What would life be like without her presence and her smiles? How could I live without her? These and other fears gripped my soul. I felt that I would lose my mind. I had never experienced such feelings of helplessness and hopelessness. I felt hopeless because I perceived she was dying; I felt helpless because I could see death taking her from me and there was nothing I could do. There was no one to accompany her on this lonesome trip. *What was I to do?* It was this same night, in October of 1986, when I experienced the unexplainable healing power of God's word.

For years, as a young Christian, I had shared God's word with people who had experienced the death of their loved ones. I had no real idea of what they could have been feeling. Now was the time for me to apply the remedy to my own hurts that I had given to countless others, the word of God. Embracing the reality of my mother's death became overwhelming. I could not think of any scriptures that could heal what I was feeling during the first couple of hours. Not only could I not think of any, at that time, I did not want to know any. *I only wanted my mother; I just wanted her to live; nothing else, I just wanted her to live.*

At some point following that two-hour span, the Holy Ghost began to draw me to the word of God. I began to read the familiar scriptures that I had shared with others who had been bereaved of their loved ones. In situations where I knew their deceased had confessed Christ, I would share with them the following scriptures in Psalms 116:15 and Revelation 14:13; they follow respectively:

The Power of Forgiveness

Precious in the sight of the LORD is the death of his saints.

And I heard a voice from heaven saying unto me, Write, Blessed are the dead-which die in the Lord from henceforth: Yea, saith the Spirit, that they may rest from their labours; and their-works do follow them.

I knew these words were true; yet, I still felt like I was loosing my mind. I kept reading those verses. Somehow, it seemed that I needed something else. I began to pray. I was open with God; I told Him that I did not feel I could make it. I admitted I was scared. At a certain point, God led me to Romans 14: 7-8:

For none of us liveth to himself, and no man dieth to himself.

For whether we live, we live unto the Lord; and whether we die, we die unto the Lord: whether we live therefore, or die, we are the Lord's.

Whatever the meaning of these verses, God knew they were sufficient for my healing at a critical time. They refocused my thinking. They got me through that horrible experience of embracing the fact that she was dying, and there was a peace that flooded my soul that same night that was as strong as the pain and fear that I had felt some four or more hours earlier. The peace I found in God's word surpassed my understanding, and it walked me through the next two weeks of my mother's cancer-stricken life. It gave me unusual strength during her death, funeral, and the perplexing days to follow.

I know I had read this passage in Romans since I had read the entire bible. Yet, I never recalled reading it before. The precious words were just what I needed for my particular situation. They began to comfort me as I accepted the fact that I had to go on without my mother and friend. The message that embraced my soul through God's word was profound. It could not have been any clearer if Jesus had spoken verbally to me, and said, "This river, I'm going to help her across." These are the words of God that spoke directly to my particular pain of perceiving that my mother was dying alone, and there was nothing I could do to help her, nor was there anyone who could accompany her on this cold, solitary trip.

God knew exactly what I needed for my situation, and He supplied it through His word; consequently, I was able to let go. After that, I was able to embrace the words that one of our faithful members, Beverly T. Wyatt, shared with me earlier during this ordeal, "Sis. Crockett, your mother trusted God to live; now, you let her trust him to die."

It is important to know that God wants to heal all our hurts, and it is equally as important to apply His word to our situations. There is healing in God's word for every hurt we will ever encounter and, especially, there is healing for you.

There is Healing in the Blood of Jesus

Since God does not find pleasure in the discomfort of His children, He sent His only begotten Son that we might have an abundance of life full of joy, peace, and health. Harboring unforgiveness hinders these manifold blessings that are ours through the death of Jesus on the cross. 1 Peter 2:24 reads:

...Who his own self bare our sins in his own body on the tree, that we, being dead to sins, should live unto righteousness: by whose stripes ye were healed.

It is by the shedded blood of the Son of God that we can receive inner healing. It is realized by believing in the redemptive work of the cross. While the word is the medium of healing, the power of the blood of Jesus Christ makes it possible. According to James 1:22-25, the healing that comes through the blood, takes place as we hear and obey God's word. Also, James 5:16 and Proverbs 28:13 let us know that acknowledging and confessing our sins and our needs are foundational for healing. They read as following:

Confess your faults one to another, and pray one for another, that ye may be healed. The effectual fervent prayer of a righteous man availeth much.

He that covereth his sins shall not prosper: but-whoso confesseth and forsaketh them shall have mercy.

Confessing does not mean that you must publicly announce what you have done or how you feel. It simply means that you acknowledge your sins when you go before God in prayer. When you have sinned and cannot find peace this may be an indication that you may need to share your feelings with a trusted friend or perhaps your leader. When one confesses or talks about something that annoys him, usually, it releases him from the guilt that has a tendency to haunt its victims who cover their sins. However, as a person of leadership in the church, if you publicly sin, you may be required to acknowledge it publicly since your behavior may have a negative impact on the ministry. 1 Timothy 5:19-20 reads as follows:

Against an elder receive not an accusation, but before two or three-witnesses.

Them that sin rebuke before all, that others also may fear.

Nevertheless, as we embrace His act of love on the cross, it will enable us to overcome the sin of unforgiveness.

CHAPTER X: RISE-UP AND DELIVER YOURSELF

🌟🌟🌟🌟🌟🌟🌟🌟🌟🌟🌟🌟🌟🌟🌟🌟🌟🌟🌟🌟🌟🌟🌟🌟🌟🌟
Don't focus on the past; what has been, has been and what has happened, has happened, therefore, look ahead at what can be.
🌟🌟🌟🌟🌟🌟🌟🌟🌟🌟🌟🌟🌟🌟🌟🌟🌟🌟🌟🌟🌟🌟🌟🌟🌟🌟

Many people harbor unforgiveness and hold others accountable for where they are. Sometimes, they feel that their parents are the cause of their ill fate. Others hold their spouses, their children, their bosses, or perhaps someone else responsible for their unfavorable situations. Nevertheless, whatever hurt you have had in the past, you have the ability to rise up and deliver yourself through the power of God. Don't focus on the past; what has been, *has been* and what has happened, *has happened,* therefore, look ahead at what *can be.*

As for myself, I will forever believe that Satan had a plan to cut me off, through my parents, before I was conceived. Just as God knew me before I was born, Satan knew me too, and his intentions were to destroy me before I came forth to carry out my divine assignment. I became very aware of this later in my spiritual walk. My mother had often shared with me the various circumstances surrounding my birth. Because of hard work in the fields coupled with the physical, mental, and emotional abuse, along with not having enough food for proper nutrients, she had several miscarriages and feeble babies. Four of the five babies born between my oldest sister and me were too weak to live, and the report was that a family member murdered the other; I was the seventh child. I was undernourished and born a preemie. According to the record, I too was not strong enough to survive. My mother said she prayed over me day and night; God spared my life; I lived, but the next baby died.

※※※※※※※※※※※※※※※※※※※※※※※※※※※※※※
Only they could have made me, and I thank them for bringing forth a daughter where all elements intersected at the very point of the proper time and place so I and only I could have been born.
※※※※※※※※※※※※※※※※※※※※※※※※※※※※※※

Earlier in the first chapter of this book, I talked about the purpose for the bittersweet life my mom lived. I resolved that there was a plan for all of her hurt and pain. While I do not know all of the reasons for the suffering she endured, I am convinced that some were designed by Satan to hinder her from giving birth to me. She was destined to marry my father, who became a weekend alcoholic and an abuser. It was necessary for my parents to be who they were and to experience what they did in order for me to be who I am. In fact, I could not and would not have been, if my father and my mother had not come together. Only *they* could have

The Power of Forgiveness

made *me, and* I thank them for bringing forth a daughter where all elements intersected at the very point of the proper time and place so I and only I could have been born.

Even though all of my experiences and circumstances could have caused me to become weak and bitter, I have become stronger and better. I believe I am a stronger and better person because of the things I have suffered. What the devil thought would destroy me, actually worked out for my good. I have learned first-hand what many hurting people feel. While I have come to know what it means to abound, I also know what it feels like to live in poverty. I know what it feels like to a young child to see his father abuse his mother. I know what it feels like to be angry and resentful of your mother. I know the feeling of having a relative to savagely hit your father in his head, and leave him by the side of the road to die, hence, causing your father and family more mental anguish and hardship. I also know what it feels like to put your life into the ministry, and to have a brother or sister to sow discord, and thus, cause the membership to suffer lost. I know the feeling of having someone you love and trust immensely to deceive you and betray your confidence. Yes, I know what it feels like to have inner hurt, but more importantly, I know the peace that comes through forgiving.

At this point, don't look for someone else to blame for your painful situation. Instead, use it to propel you to the level where you were destined to be. Remember, as you begin to forgive, you become strong in the might of God; He empowers you to mount up above the storms of your life. He enables you to travel the highways that He has charted for your course. He blesses you to walk through your valleys of pain and not faint. Your storms will toss you back and forth, but they will not destroy you.

On the highways that God has charted for your life, you will encounter obstacles. You will come to hills and mountains, but you will not be overcome. God will give you strength to climb every hill and mountain. As you go through your valleys of misfortune, you will be endowed with extraordinary courage to press on, and God will give you grace to finish your course.

Conclusion

I believe that every experience, good, beautiful, bad, and ugly, plays a role in shaping our lives for ministry. As children of God, remember that every pain can be instrumental in making you what you were born to be. Everyone born is a part of God's plan, but harboring unforgiveness diminishes our potential to be what we were born to be and to do what we were born to do. On the other hand, when you forgive, you open up a whole new dimension of inner healing for your total self. It enables you to tap into the area of your life that has been lying barren because of unforgiveness. It allows you to receive the promises that were forfeited

The Power of Forgiveness

because you failed to let go of your hurt. Forgiveness puts you on the right path to accomplishing what you are capable of accomplishing and doing what you are capable of doing. God knew our potential before we were formed in the womb. He knew the heartaches we would experience. He knew every tear that would fall from our eyes before we were born.

According to my friend Stephanie Gant in her book, *Women of Destiny Fulfilling God's Purpose,* "God is a God of great detail and order." Consequently, God took care of every tiny detail of our lives before we were born so we could complete our divine assignments. Do you know what God has ordained for you? If you do, step out and establish your faith in the word. Then, exercise the power God has given you, and expunge those overdue accounts of hurt and pain. Do not allow them to hinder you from accomplishing your mission. Instead, forgive, rise up, and deliver yourself. You have the power to rise from where you are. If you are down, get up. Open your spiritual eyes and see whom God has intended for you to be; open your spiritual ears and hear what God has prepared for you, and extend your spiritual arms to embrace your inner healing. Remember the small word, a divine concept, and a remedy for inner healing is to simply "forgive."

CHAPTER XI: PERSONAL TESTAMONIES OF HOW I FOUND COMFORT IN THE WORD OF GOD THROUGH PRAYER

In the following paragraphs, I will share testimonies that give accounts as to how I found comfort through prayer in the word. I will not go into all the details, but I merely want to let you know that there is healing in the word for whatever ails you. I can recall many times when I felt that my back was against the wall, and I did not know what to do; in fact, there was nothing I could do. During those trying times, I found comfort in God's word; I hasten to say it was during my most intimate prayer time. Unquestionably, God's word has a message that is suited for every particular need.

Testimony #1—I recall when my husband and I were involved in a situation that had an impact on our family, as well as the lives of other people. It was a strength-draining ordeal. After every meeting I was so physically drained that I had to literally stay in the bed for a day. God spoke to my spirit, and said He was our battle-ax. I immediately began to search God's word to find a scripture to substantiate these comforting words. I found in the book of Jeremiah 51:20 words that spoke to the effect that the Lord of host is my battle-ax. As I meditated on those words, I became very aware, beyond a shadow of a doubt, that God was the ax in our battle,

The Power of Forgiveness

and I felt the Holy Ghost empowering us to do what we needed to do to make a difference. Consequently, I departed from each impending meeting with a renewed sense of direction and valor.

Testimony #2—Again, when I was overwhelmed with a painful encounter, a profound healing came to me through the word of God. The Holy Spirit birthed in my spirit the scripture in Isaiah 54:17. It was revealed to me, *if I do right, that no weapon formed against me would prosper.* God made me very cognizant in my spirit that I would condemn every tongue that would rise up against me in the judgment. He assured me that this was my heritage.

I had read this passage before, but I was basically familiar with the part that stated, "No weapon that is formed against thee shall prosper." I had never paid attention to the second and third parts; it was in these two parts where my great consolation came. As I attempted to embrace the words in my spirit, at that time I was so hurt, I could not grasp the real meaning. I was literally knocked to my face in prayer as I tried to deal with the pain. I went into pray three times. I tried to make sense of how people who are trusted so much can betray and undermine your confidence. I can vividly recall God speaking to my spirit, asking, *"Do you have it?"* I said, *"No, I don't have it.* "The same thing happen as I went into prayer the second time.

Martha L. Crockett

After the third encounter in prayer, God asked me, *"Do you have it?* "I said, *"Yes, God I got it."* Actually what God was questioning me about was if I had the assurance of my heritage as a righteous servant. Only those who do right can say, "No weapon formed against me shall prosper." In fact, I saw the weapon forming against me by a person I loved dearly and trusted so much, and that's what made it so painful. Before prayer, I felt as though my life had been shattered.

Upon God assuring me of my heritage, I emerged from prayer with more courage to continue my work in the kingdom. Even to this day, when I see the enemy forming his powerful weapon of war, I am confident it will not prosper. It was those comforting words that helped me to continue my God-given assignment even when I felt like my heart was being torn. God gave me such an assurance through His word in prayer; I felt that a hedge was around me, and the devil could not get to me. For years I had quoted the scripture, but this experience gave me an occasion to live it. After such an encounter, I found comfort in the word of God that no weapon formed against me would prosper; this is my heritage as a righteous servant.

Testimony #3—On another occasion, the enemy began to form one of his powerful forces. The situation got ugly. God spoke a comforting word to my spirit. He inspired me with the knowledge that *He was at my back, and my front; He was at my right side and my left.* I said, "My God, with a God like this around me, I

The Power of Forgiveness

don't have any reason to fear." Also, while I was in prayer, God's Spirit moved on me to write an official complaint. I took it to the institution. As I walked in, I felt God all around me, I asked to speak to the head person; I felt like I owned the company because I knew God was with me, and we made the majority. Psalms 34:7 says, the angel of the Lord encamps around those who fear the Lord and delivers them. There is no doubt that God was already fighting my battle even before I knew there was a weapon being formed and a battle to fight. I hasten to say He had it all in control, and He delivered me from the hands of my enemy.

Testimony #4—It seems that when God begins to bless the ministry in a mighty way, the devil gets very busy. On one such occasion, he launched a strong spiritual warfare. I had an encounter with a controlling spirit for about three months. One day as I was in prayer, the Holy Spirit began to minister to me. I was given specific directions and I followed them completely. God delivered me the same day. After my confrontation with this spirit, God birthed in my mind; *The devil can't touch you.* God made me very conscience that no force could stop what He had begun; neither could it destroy what He had established. Jesus lets us know that those whom God has given him, no man can pluck them out of his hands. John 10:27-29 reads as follows:

> *My sheep hear my voice, and I know them, and they follow me: And I give unto them eternal*

life; and they shall never perish, neither shall any man pluck them out of my hand.

My Father, which gave them me, is greater than all; and no man is able to pluck them out of my Father's hand.

I knew my husband and I were in God's hands, and *the devil couldn't touch us.* Not only was I convinced that *the devil couldn't touch us,* I was also assured that God is all around us. I was persuaded in my mind that God is our battle-ax and I knew beyond a shadow of a doubt that no weapon formed against us would prosper. All of these comforting words came back overflowing my soul as God ministered to my spirit as I reflected upon my encounter with this evil force.

It is very important that when you don't know what you need, or you don't know what to do, to prayerfully seek God through His word concerning your particular hurt. He will give you comfort, and He will give you directions.

APPENDIX

Self Development Activities

I have found the exercises outlined below helpful in my quest for inner healing. If you are experiencing inner hurt but want to experience the healing power of forgiveness, I challenge you to take a leap of faith. Complete the self-development activities below, and prayerfully, you will begin the process of inner healing.

Exercise 1

Take a day or so to write down all the ugly feelings you have about any person, place, or thing. Be open with yourself. If you feel really ugly about it, write it down.

Whatever you feel, just write it. Ask God to help you identify your feelings. This activity can help you recognize if you are hurting. Take some time to think about what you have written. Once you feel that you have resolved what your feelings are, you are ready to move to the next step.

Exercise 2

Using the same sheet of paper, write down why you feel the way you do about the person, place, or object. Try to be specific and write exactly what causes you to feel the way you do. This activity can help you begin to identify what caused your hurt.

Exercise 3

Look at your list from Exercise 2. Analyze everything you have written. On a separate sheet of paper, write down the specific experience from your list that caused your hurt. Be sure that you write down the specific act/acts that hurt you deeply. If you carefully analyze your feelings, you are more than likely to determine the root of your pain. Once you have determined who and/or what hurt you, you are in a position to begin your healing process.

Exercise 4

This activity may take more than a day. It may take weeks, months or longer. The important thing is that you accept the reality of your pain. Don't try to act like you are not hurt. Talk to a trusted person about your feelings. If you have had a very painful encounter, talk to someone. There is someone who can help you. A good place to start seeking help is with your pastor or a spiritual counselor. You may need a psychiatrist or some other trained medical professional. Don't keep your feelings bogged up inside of you. Don't accept the lie the devil has told you that people will not like you if they know your real story. Also, accept that there is healing for you. This is your leap of faith.

Exercise 5

Once you come to understand that you are really hurt, you must resolve to let go.

You may not be able to let go all at once, but at least when you decide to, you can begin to move toward your healing. God looks at your heart. He knows that it takes time for you to let go of some of your pain. The important thing is you must have a forgiving heart. As you begin to forgive others, God will begin to forgive you. Jesus taught his disciples in the model prayer to pray in Matthews 6:12, "Forgive us our debts as we forgive our debtors." Prayer is the key to getting through this stage.

It does not matter how long it takes to get through this step, don't give up. Your healing comes through being able to let go. To let go is to forgive, and you cannot let go unless you forgive. Pray and ask God to help you to forgive those who have deeply hurt you. Ask God to help you to get through this activity. Prayer is the key to this step. Pray your way through. If you can do nothing else, pray until something happens. If nothing happens, keep praying. Prayer will change you. Prayer will change the way you think, feel, and act. It will impact your life. It will bring you into the very presence of God. In the presence of God, is a treasure of healing. More importantly, there is healing for you!

ABOUT THE AUTHOR

Martha has been in the ministry for more than forty years. This book, which is her first, is a credit to her experiences. She is gifted in the healing ministries, and she has a message for the emotionally wounded.

Martha has a B.S. Degree in Accounting and Finances and a Master in Business Education from Virginia State University. She closed her accounting practice, and stopped her pursuit of a career in public education to concentrate her energies in the work of the ministry.

Martha is married to her predestined mate, Herman Crockett, Jr.; they have been happily married for over 33 years. They have four beautiful daughters, who are active in ministry, Tabitha, Sheree, and Mikela. They have one son-in-law and four beautiful grandchildren —Courtenay, Tiffani, Wayne and Jayla.

email address: MLEAN725@aol.com

Phone number-804.861.3898
Fax 804-861-3884

Correspondence may be directed to: Faith and Hope Temple Church of God in Christ
1800 East Washington Street
Petersburg, VA 23803